Contents

KU-146-214

Introduction

Who is this book for?

Speaking for IELTS will prepare you for the IELTS Speaking test whether you are taking the test for the first time, or re-sitting. It has been written for learners with band score 5–5.5 who are trying to achieve band score 6 or higher.

The structured approach, comprehensive answer key and sample answers have been designed so that you can use the materials to study on your own. However, the book can also be used as a supplementary speaking skills course for IELTS preparation classes. The book provides enough material for approximately 50 hours of classroom activity.

Content

Speaking for IELTS is divided into 12 units. Each unit focuses on a topic area that you are likely to meet in the IELTS exam. This helps you to build up a bank of vocabulary and ideas related to a variety of the topics.

Units 1–11 cover vocabulary, grammar, pronunciation and exam techniques to prepare you for the IELTS Speaking test. Every exercise is relevant to the test. The aims listed at the start of each unit specify the key skills, techniques and language covered in the unit. You work towards Unit 12, which provides a final practice IELTS Speaking test.

Additionally, the book provides examination strategies telling you what to expect and how best to succeed in the test. Exam information is presented in clear, easy-to-read chunks. 'Exam tips' in each unit highlight essential exam techniques and can be rapidly reviewed at a glance.

Unit structure

Each of the first 11 units is divided into 2 parts.

The **first part** of each unit introduces vocabulary related to the topic, as well as phrases and language that can be applied to any topic. The vocabulary exercises give you the opportunity to express complex ideas and opinions so that you are able to do so in the IELTS Speaking test. The vocabulary is presented using Collins COBUILD dictionary definitions. In addition, each unit covers one or more pronunciation points, and one or more grammar points. The pronunciation and grammar exercises help you to develop accurate pronunciation, and grammatical range and accuracy to enable you to succeed in the IELTS test.

In every unit, you are given the opportunity to practise the new language you have learnt by attempting questions from Part 1, Part 2 and Part 3 of the IELTS Speaking test. These test questions increase your familiarity with the exam format and help to build your confidence.

The **second part** of each unit teaches you exam techniques. The information and exercises raise your awareness of what constitutes an effective IELTS response and also provide you with strategies on how to achieve this. Techniques include making notes for Part 2 of the IELTS Speaking test, developing your fluency, and enhancing the length and quality of your answers to Part 3 of the test by using news articles.

Answer key

A comprehensive answer key is provided for all sections of the book including recommended answers and explanations. You will also find full audio scripts of all speaking exercises at the back of the book. There are sample answers for all the IELTS Speaking test questions recorded on the CDs. The audio scripts for these sample answers are also at the back of the book. Listening to and learning from these will help you to achieve the best scores.

Using the book for self-study

If you are new to IELTS, we recommend that you work systematically through the 12 units in order to benefit from the book's progressive structure. If you are a more experienced learner, you can use the aims listed at the start of each unit to select the most useful exercises.

Each unit contains between three and four hours of study material. Having access to someone who can provide informed feedback on the speaking practice exercises is an advantage. However, you can still learn a lot working alone or with a study partner willing to give and receive peer feedback.

Avoid writing the answers to vocabulary exercises directly into the book so that you can try the exercises again once you have completed the unit. As you attempt the exercises in each unit, write down in a separate notebook any language that you find particularly useful or relevant. Review this language often.

Try to revise what you have learnt before attempting the practice IELTS questions in each unit. This will improve the quality of your answers, and using the new language will help you to remember it.

Record your answers if you can. It will develop your self-awareness: you will be able to hear where your strengths lie and which aspects of your speaking you need to improve. In addition, hearing how your speaking has improved over time will increase your confidence and motivation. Remember that there are no 'right' or 'wrong' answers to the exam questions: the examiner is interested in your English, not in testing the validity of your opinions.

Once you have answered the practice IELTS questions, listen to the sample answers. You can also read the sample answers in the audio scripts section at the back of the book. Write down any useful vocabulary and grammatical structures. Be aware that 'vocabulary' consists of more than just single words: also pay attention to bigger chunks of language, such as phrases and collocations.

It is recommended that you play the sample answers a second time. This time, read the words as you listen, imitating as closely as possible the native speakers' pronunciation.

It is very important that you do not memorise entire sentences or answers. IELTS examiners are trained to spot this and will change the topic if they think you are repeating memorised answers. With its structured approach, wide range of relevant exercises, and exam tips and techniques, *Speaking for IELTS* should equip you with the skills and language, as well as the confidence, necessary to tackle unfamiliar questions on the day of the exam.

Unit 12 is a complete practice speaking test. This unit should be done under exam conditions including setting yourself the time limits that are suggested. There is also a sample answer for this complete practice test so you can listen to the audio and read the audio script to further learn from the experience of sitting this practice test.

The International English Language Testing System (IELTS) Test

IELTS is jointly managed by the British Council, Cambridge ESOL Examinations and IDP Education, Australia.

There are two versions of the test:

- Academic
- General Training

Academic is for students wishing to study at undergraduate or postgraduate levels in an English-medium environment.

General Training is for people who wish to migrate to an English-speaking country.

The Test

There are four modules:

Listening	30 minutes, plus 10 minutes for transferring answers to the answer sheet NB: the audio is heard *only once*. Approx. 10 questions per section Section 1: two speakers discuss a social situation Section 2: one speaker talks about a non-academic topic Section 3: up to four speakers discuss an educational project Section 4: one speaker gives a talk of general academic interest
Reading	60 minutes 3 texts, taken from authentic sources, on general, academic topics. They may contain diagrams, charts, etc. 40 questions: may include multiple choice, sentence completion, completing a diagram, graph or chart, choosing headings, yes/no, true/false questions, classification and matching exercises.
Writing	Task 1: 20 minutes: description of a table, chart, graph or diagram (150 words minimum) Task 2: 40 minutes: an essay in response to an argument or problem (250 words minimum)
Speaking	11–14 minutes A three-part face-to-face oral interview with an examiner. The interview is recorded. Part 1: introductions and general questions (4–5 mins) Part 2: individual long turn (3–4 mins) – the candidate is given a task, has one minute to prepare, then talks for 1–2 minutes, with some questions from the examiner. Part 3: two-way discussion (4–5 mins): the examiner asks further questions on the topic from Part 2, and gives the candidate the opportunity to discuss more abstract issues or ideas.
Timetabling	Listening, Reading and Writing must be taken on the same day, and in the order listed above. Speaking can be taken up to 7 days before or after the other modules.
Scoring	Each section is given a band score. The average of the four scores produces the Overall Band Score. You do not pass or fail IELTS; you receive a score.

IELTS and the Common European Framework of Reference

The CEFR shows the level of the learner and is used for many English as a Foreign Language examinations. The table below shows the approximate CEFR level and the equivalent IELTS Overall Band Score:

CEFR description	CEFR code	IELTS Band Score
Proficient user (Advanced)	C2 C1	9 7–8
Independent user (Intermediate – Upper Intermediate)	B2 B1	5–6.5 4–5

This table contains the general descriptors for the band scores 1–9:

IELTS Band Scores		
9	Expert user	Has fully operational command of the language: appropriate, accurate and fluent with complete understanding.
8	Very good user	Has fully operational command of the language, with only occasional unsystematic inaccuracies and inappropriacies. Misunderstandings may occur in unfamiliar situations. Handles complex detailed argumentation well.
7	Good user	Has operational command of the language, though with occasional inaccuracies, inappropriacies and misunderstandings in some situations. Generally handles complex language well and understands detailed reasoning.
6	Competent user	Has generally effective command of the language despite some inaccuracies, inappropriacies and misunderstandings. Can use and understand fairly complex language, particularly in familiar situations.
5	Modest user	Has partial command of the language, coping with overall meaning in most situations, though is likely to make many mistakes. Should be able to handle basic communication in own field.
4	Limited user	Basic competence is limited to familiar situations. Has frequent problems in understanding and expression. Is not able to use complex language.
3	Extremely limited user	Conveys and understands only general meaning in very familiar situations. Frequent breakdowns in communication occur.
2	Intermittent user	No real communication is possible except for the most basic information using isolated words or short formulae in familiar situations and to meet immediate needs. Has great difficulty understanding spoken and written English.
1	Non-user	Essentially has no ability to use the language beyond possibly a few isolated words.
0	Did not attempt the test	No assessable information provided.

Marking

The Listening and Reading papers have 40 items, each worth one mark if correctly answered. Here are some examples of how marks are translated into band scores:

Listening: 16 out of 40 correct answers: band score 5
             23 out of 40 correct answers: band score 6
             30 out of 40 correct answers: band score 7

Reading   15 out of 40 correct answers: band score 5
             23 out of 40 correct answers: band score 6
             30 out of 40 correct answers: band score 7

Writing and Speaking are marked according to performance descriptors.
Writing: examiners award a band score for each of four areas with equal weighting:

• Task achievement (Task 1)
• Task response (Task 2)
• Coherence and cohesion
• Lexical resource and grammatical range and accuracy

Speaking: examiners award a band score for each of four areas with equal weighting:

• Fluency and coherence
• Lexical resource
• Grammatical range
• Accuracy and pronunciation

For full details of how the examination is scored and marked, go to: www.ielts.org

1 People & relationships

Aims: Describing personality | Talking about relationships
Using tenses correctly | Pronunciation: Strong and weak forms of prepositions
Exam technique: What it means to 'know' a word

Vocabulary: Character and personality

1   Use a dictionary to find the meanings of the adjectives describing character and
personality below.

ambitious	good fun	nosy	reliable
blunt	hard-working	open-minded	self-assured
clever	impatient	outgoing	sociable
creative	judgemental	over-sensitive	stingy

2 Which adjectives in Exercise 1 are negative and which are positive? Draw a table like the one below and put the words into the correct column.

Positive	Negative

3 Which adjectives from Exercise 1 would you use to describe yourself?

I consider myself to be _____.

I would say I was _____.

Vocabulary: Relationships

4 Match phrases 1–8 with definitions a–h.

1	get on with somebody	a	argue and stop being friendly with somebody
2	look up to somebody	b	have a good relationship
3	be in touch with somebody	c	gradually have a less close relationship with somebody
4	fall out with somebody	d	be in communication with somebody
5	grow apart from somebody	e	know somebody well and see or talk to them often
6	take after somebody	f	have many childhood and adolescent experiences in common with somebody
7	grow up together/with somebody	g	respect somebody
8	be close to somebody	h	resemble somebody in your family (in appearance or personality)

5 Using phrases from Exercise 4, make eight sentences describing relationships you have.

Example: I take after my dad – we're both quite careless.

6 Listen to three people talk about their relatives. Make notes as you listen. How do they describe their relatives and their relationships with them?

01
CD1

1 _____

2 _____

3 _____

Listen again and make more notes. Look up any language you do not know in your dictionary and make a note of it.

Vocabulary: Modifying

7 Listen to Track 1 again and notice how the adjectives describing character and personality are modified. Complete sentences 1–10 with the modifying adverbs you hear.

01
CD1

1 She's _____ outgoing and sociable.

2 She's _____ hard-working.

3 She can be _____ impatient.

4 He was _____ creative.

5 He's not _____ reliable.

6 She's _____ nosy.

7 She's _____ blunt.

8 She can be _____ stingy.

9 She's _____ clever.

10 She's _____ self-assured and ambitious.

8 Read the following guidance on modifying adjectives.

1 We can use adverbs like *really* and *so* before a positive adjective.

Example: *She's really outgoing.*

He was so creative.

2 We can use the same adverbs before a negative adjective, but we normally do this only if we do not like the person or are angry with them.

Example: *She's so nosy.*

3 If we say something negative about someone, e.g. *She is impatient*, or *He is unreliable*, it can sound rude or too direct. We often 'soften' negative comments for this reason. Here are two ways of doing this:

• with *can be a bit*

Example: *She can be a bit impatient.*

• with *not very* + a positive adjective

Example: *He's not very reliable.*

9 Listen to Track 1 again and repeat. Pay particular attention to your pronunciation.

01
CD1

> **Exam tip:** If you use a character adjective to describe someone in the exam, you should expand on it or explain it.
>
> *Examples:*
>
> *She's really outgoing and sociable – she's always going out with friends and colleagues.*
>
> *He's not very reliable, so, for example, if I email him, he won't respond.*
>
> *She's terribly blunt, which means she quite often upsets us with the things she says.*

10 Write descriptions, similar to those you heard in Track 1, of four members of your family. Use some of the adjectives from Part 1 of this unit. Remember to modify the adjectives and explain or expand on each characteristic. Include at least one negative point for each person.

11 To practise your speaking skills and help you to remember the vocabulary you have learnt, tell an English-speaking friend about your relatives, or record yourself. Do not write down what you want to say and read it out; you will not be able to do that in the exam. You must not memorize whole sentences or whole answers. You must speak spontaneously.

 Exam information
Part 1: Introduction and interview (4–5 minutes)
In Part 1 of the Exam, the examiner will introduce him/herself and ask you to introduce yourself and confirm your identity. The examiner will then ask you general questions on three familiar topic areas. The first topic will be *Studies*, *Work* or *Where you live*. In each unit of this book, you will practise answering Part 1 questions on one topic.

Part 1 tests your ability to communicate opinions and information on everyday topics and common experiences.

'02
CD1

IELTS Speaking Exam: Part 1

12 You are going to hear questions that are typical of Part 1 of the exam. Listen to each question and give your answer. Try to use some of the vocabulary and language you have learnt in this unit.

Now listen to the sample answers.

 Exam information
Part 2: Individual long turn (3–4 minutes)
The examiner will give you a task card that asks you to talk about a particular topic and includes points that you can cover in your talk. You do not have to cover all the points and you do not have to talk about them in order. You will be given one minute to prepare your talk, and you will be given a pencil and paper to make notes (do not write on the task card). You must talk for one to two minutes on the topic. The examiner will then ask you one or two questions on the same topic.

Part 2 tests your ability to talk at length, organising your ideas coherently.

IELTS Speaking Exam: Part 2

13 Read this Part 2 question. Give yourself one minute to plan your answer, making notes if you wish. Then talk for one to two minutes. Remember: you can use the vocabulary you have learnt in this unit to talk about friendship too.

Describe a close friend.

You should say:

    how long you have known this person

    how you met

    what kind of person he/she is

and explain why you like him/her.

Grammar: Thinking about tenses

14 Read the Part 2 Exam questions from Exercise 13 again.

1 How long have you known this person?

2 How did you meet?

3 What kind of person is he/she?

4 Explain why you like him/her.

Judging from the tenses used in each question, which tenses are you likely to use in your responses?

> **Exam tip:** In the exam, look carefully at the tenses used in the Part 2 questions, and listen carefully to the examiner to hear which tenses they use in their questions. Does the question relate to the past, present, future, or something imagined? This will help you use the correct tenses when you speak.

03
CD1

15 Listen to the sample answer to the Part 2 Exam question in Exercise 13. Then read the extracts below. What tenses does the speaker use and why does he use those tenses?

1 We got to know each other on the tennis courts. _____

2 He'd often suggest doing something and I'd go along with it. _____

3 We've never fallen out. _____

16 Now answer the Part 2 Exam question in Exercise 13 again, aiming for accuracy in your use of tenses.

Pronunciation: Weak and strong forms

17 Some words have two pronunciations: a strong form and a weak form. In normal speech, we usually use the weak form as in the sentences below. Look at sentences 1–5, and circle the prepositions.

1 Can I have a cup of tea?

2 We met at uni.

3 I've known him for ten years.

4 I'm from Dubai.

5 It's quarter to ten.

04
CD1

18 Do you know the weak forms of the prepositions in Exercise 17? Listen and repeat, taking care not to stress the weak forms.

> **Exam tip:** If you use weak forms correctly, you will be more fluent and you will sound more like a native speaker. This will get you higher marks in the exam.
>
> Knowing about weak forms will also help you understand the examiner more easily; it is easy to miss weak forms because they are unstressed.

19 Look at the table below. Listen and repeat the strong and weak prepositions. Note that *to* and *for* have different weak forms when they come before vowel sounds.

You will find a full guide to reading phonetic symbols at the back of this book.

Word	Strong form	Weak form(s)	Weak form before a vowel sound
1 to	/tuː/	/tə/	/tʊ/ e.g. I'm going to Egypt.
2 of	/ɒv/	/əv/, /ə/	—
3 at	/æt/	/ət/	—
4 from	/frɒm/	/frəm/	—
5 for	/fɔː/	/fə/	/fər/ e.g. This is for Andy.

20 Sometimes, even in fast speech, we use the strong form of a word:

a if we want to emphasise it, or contrast it with another word

b if it comes before a pause

c if it comes at the end of a sentence

Listen to sentences 1–4. Are the prepositions strong or weak? If they are strong, give a reason from the list a–c above.

1 Has she been waiting for long? _____

2 What are you looking at? _____

3 The present's not from Mark, it's for Mark. _____

4 I want to go! _____

Now check your answers. Then repeat the sentences.

> **Exam tip:** Other function words (or grammatical words) also have weak forms. Some common ones are:
>
> • positive auxiliary verbs (e.g. *can, must, do, shall, was, are*)
> • pronouns (e.g. *her, you, them, your*)
> • conjunctions (e.g. *and, but, because ('cos), than*)
> • articles (*the, a, an*)
>
> A good dictionary will give you guidance on strong and weak pronunciations.
>
> Practise using weak forms by saying sentences that have prepositions in them.

Exam technique: What it means to 'know' a word

> **Exam tip:** In the IELTS Speaking exam you will be judged on your use of vocabulary. Having a good vocabulary is not just about knowing lots of words and phrases. You have to know how to use them. If you use slang in the exam, it might sound inappropriate. Equally, some words that are extremely formal or old-fashioned are not often used in speaking, and might also sound inappropriate.

1 Match words 1–5 with their more neutral synonyms a–e. Which of the words 1–5 are informal and which are old-fashioned?

1	mate	a	parents
2	beau	b	boyfriend
3	bloke	c	friend
4	folks	d	members of a family
5	kinsfolk	e	man

2 To really *know* a piece of vocabulary, you should know the following:

1 What part of speech is it? For example, what part of speech is *folks*? What part of speech is *formal*?

2 What are the other parts of speech of the word? For example: *formalise*. (v)

3 Is the word slang, informal, formal, or old-fashioned? Is it used in all English-speaking countries or just in some countries? For example, is *bloke* used in the UK or the US?

4 Does the word have any connotations you should be aware of? For example, both *slim* and *skinny* mean *thin*, but which can be insulting and which is complimentary?

5 How do you pronounce the word, and which syllable is stressed? For example, which syllable is stressed in *boyfriend*? Which syllable is stressed in *acquaintance*?

6 Note the grammar of the word/phrase. Is it an irregular verb (for example, *seek–sought–sought*) or a noun with an irregular plural (for example, *man–men*)? Is it followed by a particular preposition?

7 Are there any useful collocations? For example, you know the word *friend*, but do you know and use all these collocations: *a close friend, make friends (with somebody), a circle of friends*. Do you know any other collocations with *friend*?

Use a dictionary to find answers to the questions in points 1–7.

3 Make notes about the words 1–3 using the guidance in Exercise 2. Use a dictionary to find/check your answers.

1 in-laws

2 other half

3 sibling

Exam information
Part 3: Two-way discussion (4–5 minutes)
The questions in Part 3 will be connected to the topic of Part 2. They allow you to discuss more abstract issues and ideas. Part 3 is a discussion between you and the examiner. In the units of this book you will hear typical Part 3 questions and practise answering them.

Part 3 tests your ability to express and justify opinions, and to analyse, discuss and speculate.

07
CD1

IELTS Speaking Exam: Part 3

4 You are going to hear questions that are typical of Part 3 of the exam. Record yourself answering the questions.

Listen to your responses. Try to judge your use of vocabulary, and ask an English-speaking friend to help you if you like.

- Was your vocabulary appropriate, or did you use some very informal or old-fashioned language?
- Did you use a good range of vocabulary, or did you use the same words repeatedly?

To enrich your vocabulary, find appropriate synonyms for five or more words or phrases. The best way to find new vocabulary is in context, such as in the sample answers in this unit or in an article or book.

Listen to the sample answer. Then answer the Part 3 questions again using these new words.

2   A healthy body

Aims: Talking about fitness, sports, health and diet
Pronunciation: Expressing enthusiasm | Expressing opinions | Collocations
Exam technique: Planning your answer

Vocabulary: Sports and fitness

1   **Underline the phrases in sentences 1–3 that best describe your lifestyle or the lifestyle of people in your country.**

  1   Most people in my country *think it is important to keep fit/don't really do anything specific to keep in shape.*

  2   I keep fit by *going jogging/going to the gym/walking everywhere.*

  3   *I work out all the time./I'm quite an active person./I never do any exercise.*

2   **Underline the words or phrases in sentences 1–3 that best describe how you feel about sport.**

  1   Watching sport is *tedious/entertaining/all right if there's nothing else on TV.*

  2   Playing sport is *exhilarating/good fun/exhausting/a great way to keep fit.*

  3   I'm *quite into sport/fanatical about sport/not the least bit interested in sport.*

3   **Write three examples of the types of sport 1–5.**

  1   contact sports   _____   _____   _____

  2   water sports   _____   _____   _____

  3   extreme sports   _____   _____   _____

  4   team sports   _____   _____   _____

  5   individual sports   _____   _____

4 Which sports do you most enjoy watching or playing, and which do you least enjoy? Why? Practise giving your answer.

🎧 5 Listen to the person on Track 08 talking about a sport.

08
CD1

1 Which sport is he talking about? _____

2 Listen again and answer questions a–f below.

   a What phrasal verb means *increases gradually*? _____

   b What is a synonym for *supporters*? _____

   c What verb means *have the same number of points or goals at the end of the game*? _____

   d What two words are used to describe where this sport is played? _____

   e Which phrase means *scored the goal that won the match*? _____

   f What phrase is used to describe someone who is likely to be very successful in the near future? _____

3 What other words and phrases does the person use to talk about the sport?

4 Listen again and make notes. Then read Track 08 on page 100 and use your dictionary to check your answers.

6 Look at the card below. Create a similar card for your own favourite sport and a second one for the most popular sport in your country (if this is different from your own favourite sport). You can find information about the sport(s) on the Internet, as well as in books, magazines and newspapers.

Tennis

Where is it played? on a tennis court

What equipment is needed to play it? a racquet, tennis balls

What is the most important event associated with this sport? Wimbledon, held in London every summer

Terminology and phrases used to talk about the sport

Describing the shots: serve, volley, smash, forehand, backhand, on the line, out

Scoring: point, game, set, match

People: player, umpire, ball boy/girl, trainer/coach

Useful phrases: He/She's broken his/her opponent's serve. He/She's served an ace. It's gone to a tie-break. What a great shot! He/She's serving for the match.

Why do you/the people in your country like this sport? It's a battle of the mind as much as the body. I find it interesting to see how some players may be highly skilled but don't have the mental strength to win.

Vocabulary: Health and diet

7 Read the definitions of *diet* below. Notice that it has two distinct meanings.

Definition a If you are on a diet, you eat special kinds of food or you eat less food than usual because you are trying to lose weight.

Definition b Your diet is the type and range of food that you regularly eat.

1 Read sentences 1–3. Which definition of *diet* applies in each sentence?

  1 I fear I have quite a poor diet.
  2 I think I have a balanced diet.
  3 I plan to go on a diet in the new year.

3 Discuss questions 1–3 with a friend, or record yourself giving your answers.

  1 Would you say you had a balanced diet? Explain why (not).
  2 Do you eat a lot of junk food? What do you (not) like about it?
  3 Have you ever been on a diet? If so, what kind of diet was it and did it work? If you haven't been on a diet, explain why not.

8 Read definitions 1–10 and then complete the words and phrases related to health and diet. There is one space per letter. Some letters have been given to help you.

  1 physically weak because you do not eat enough food or do not eat the right kind of food: ma _ _ _ _ _ _ _ _ _ _

  2 the way that chemical processes in your body cause food to be used in an efficient way, for example, to make new cells and to give you energy: me _ _ _ _ _ _ _ _

  3 substances, found in certain kinds of food, that provide you with energy: ca _ _ _ _ _ _ _ _ _ _ _

  4 substances that you need in order to remain healthy, which are found in food or can be eaten in the form of pills: vi _ _ _ _ _ _

  5 units used to measure the energy value of food: ca _ _ _ _ _ _

  6 an attempt to lose a lot of weight quickly by strictly limiting how much you eat: a c _ _ _ _   d _ _ _

  7 (of a person) become heavier: p _ _   o _   w _ _ _ _ _

  8 (of a person) become lighter: l _ _ _   w _ _ _ _ _

  9 extremely fat: ob _ _ _

  10 too thin, and therefore not healthy: un _ _ _ _ _ _ _ _ _

9 Complete sentences 1–6 using the vocabulary above.

  1 Going on _____ can be extremely dangerous. You can end up becoming _____ and be too weak to go about your daily life.

  2 Athletes eat _____ prior to a race because their bodies convert them into energy.

  3 Most people lead a sedentary lifestyle these days and ingest far more _____ than their bodies need. This means they can easily become _____.

  4 There are certain people who have such a fast _____ that it seems they don't _____ no matter how much they eat.

  5 The number of _____ models you see in magazines and on the catwalk leads many women to want to _____ themselves.

  6 Fruit and vegetables are a great source of _____.

IELTS Speaking Exam: Part 1

10 You are going to hear questions that are typical of Part 1 of the exam. Listen to each question and give your answer. Record yourself if you can.

Now listen to the sample answers. (See also Track 09, page 100.)

> **Exam tip:** You can exploit the vocabulary you wrote in the card in Exercise 6 in different ways. For example, you might be asked about a time when you won a game, and then you can use the vocabulary to talk about how you played and won a match. Or you may be asked to describe a famous person you admire. Then you could describe a sporting hero and talk about their skill in their sport and a time when they beat an opponent. Always think about how you can transfer vocabulary you have learnt to other exam questions.

IELTS Speaking Exam: Part 2

11 Read the Part 2 question below. It asks about a 'competition or sporting event', so you do not have to talk about sport if you are not interested in it. You could talk about another kind of competition, perhaps one that is traditional or popular in your country. For example, a chess tournament, a singing competition, a beauty pageant, a dancing competition, a strongest man competition, or a debating contest.

Give yourself one minute to plan your answer, making notes if you wish. Then talk for one to two minutes.

> Describe an exciting competition or sporting event you have witnessed.
>
> You should say:
>
> what the competition or sporting event was
>
> when and where it took place
>
> who won
>
> and explain why it was exciting.

Pronunciation: Expressing enthusiasm

12 Listen to four people talking about sport.

1 Who sounds enthusiastic and who sounds bored?

Speaker 1 sounds _____. Speaker 3 sounds _____.

Speaker 2 sounds _____. Speaker 4 sounds _____.

2 How did you decide who sounds enthusiastic and who sounds bored?

3 Some of the people are using language like *Oh great! Fantastic*, but they are not enthusiastic. Why do you think they are using this kind of language?

4 Intonation is the 'melody' of language. Listen to the people again and imitate their intonation.

13 Read the following on how to express enthusiasm.

> We can express enthusiasm by using:
>
> - expressive language
>   *Example: It was amazing! The crowd went wild!*
>
> - eye contact and body language
>   Look the examiner in the eye as you speak. When you are enthusiastic, your body language is more dynamic than usual: you may sit forward in your seat, widen your eyes and use your hands.
>
> - stress and intonation
>   To express enthusiasm, you should put *extra* emphasis on the stressed syllables of the most important words, saying them more slowly and more loudly than the other words. In an emphatic statement, the intonation tends to rise high and then fall dramatically.

11
CD1

14 Listen to the speaker expressing enthusiasm without using words. Copy the speaker, using body language, too. This will help you focus on expressing enthusiasm by using your voice and body rather than just certain words. Expressing intense emotions may make you feel self-conscious, so practising before the exam with a friend will help you.

12
CD1

15 Now listen to the same sentences with words. Repeat the sentences, imitating the speaker's intonation. The syllables with the most stress are in capitals.

1 It was aMAzing!
2 It was inCREdible!

3 It was BREATHtaking!
4 The crowd went WILD!

> **Exam tip:** The correct intonation – intonation that reflects accurately how you feel – will improve your marks. If you are telling an exciting story, but your intonation makes you sound bored, the examiner will probably find your story less interesting.
>
> We use different intonation to express different emotions. The best way to improve your intonation is to listen to *how* English-speakers say something, as well as *what* they say. You could watch a film and listen carefully to how the characters sound when they are sad, happy, frightened, and so on. Pause the film and imitate them.

16 Record yourself answering the Part 2 questions in Exercise 11 in your own language. Listen to yourself. How did you express your feelings of enthusiasm? Does your language express enthusiasm differently from English?

17 Listen to a sample answer to the Part 2 question in Exercise 11. Then read Track 13, page 101 and underline the language used to convey the excitement of the event. Is there anything you could have used in your own answer?
13
CD1

18 Answer the Part 2 Exam questions again and record your answer. Try and improve on your first performance by showing enthusiasm and using appropriate intonation. It will help if you try and remember your feelings when you watched the competition, and express how you felt. Do your best to sound and look enthusiastic when you are telling the most exciting parts of your story, and when you use expressions like *It was incredible!*

Expressing opinions

19   There are many phrases that indicate we are expressing an opinion, the most simple of which is probably *I think* ... Think of at least four more phrases.

Here are four more ways of giving your opinion.

a   If you ask me, ...

b   In my view, ...

c   I would argue that ...

d   I would say ...

Now express your opinion using phrases a–d above to complete sentences 1–4. Explain your opinions.

1   ... the most interesting sport is ...

2   ... the best sport for keeping fit is ...

3   ... the most difficult sport is ...

4   ... the most dangerous sport is ...

20   There are a number of useful phrases you can use when you want to give your views on controversial topics. Try creating sentences using some of these.

a   I (strongly) believe that ...

b   As far as I'm concerned, ...

c   I'm (strongly) against ...

d   I'm (strongly) in favour of ...

e   I'm convinced that would work because ...

f   I'm not convinced that would work because ...

g   I'm sceptical of the idea that ...

h   I must admit, I think ...

21   Read the proposed government schemes 1–5 and respond to them using phrases a–h above.

Your government wants to:

1   tax people who are unfit to help pay for their health care

2   make all children do at least one hour of sport a day

3   tax smokers because they have more health problems than non-smokers

4   run a campaign informing people what comprises a balanced diet

5   raise the minimum age for alcohol consumption by five years.

> **Exam tip:** Try and use a wide range of phrases for giving your opinion; this will help improve your mark.

IELTS Speaking Exam: Part 3

22 You are going to hear questions that are typical of Part 3 of the exam. Listen to each question and give your answer.

Now listen to the sample answer. Note down any useful vocabulary, then answer the Part 3 questions again using that vocabulary.

Vocabulary: Collocations

Collocations are words that are often found together. Using them will make your English sound more natural. You should not just learn isolated words; you should also look for new collocations and make a note of them.

23 Complete sentences 1–10 with the words a–j that collocate with the words in italics.

a balanced	**c** keep	**e** lead	**g** places	**i** sense
b form	**d** keep	**f** passive	**h** play	**j** set

1 The best way to _____ *fit* is to do exercise that raises your heart rate.

2 Golf, in my opinion, is not the best _____ *of exercise*.

3 You can have fun while exercising if you _____ *volleyball* with your friends a few times a week.

4 Without a TV people are much more likely to _____ *active*.

5 Parents should _____ *a good example* to their children as far as exercise is concerned.

6 Schools can teach children about eating a _____ *diet*.

7 Children will love the _____ *of achievement* sport can give you.

8 People ought to be encouraged to _____ *healthy lives*.

9 Even if you don't smoke yourself, _____ *smoking* can harm your health.

10 People should not be allowed to smoke in *public* _____.

24 Look at the different types of collocation in the table. Then draw a table like the one below and write the collocations from Exercise 23 in the correct column.

Verb + adjective	Verb + noun	Verb + adjective + noun	Noun + noun	Adjective + noun

Now find collocations related to sport and health and add them to the table. You can look for collocations in the other sample answers as well as in newspaper or magazine articles and online.

25 Answer the Part 3 questions in Exercise 22 again. This time try to use some of the collocations you have learnt.

Exam technique: Planning your answer

> **Exam tip:** When planning your answer to Part 2, remember that you do not have to cover all the points on the task card and you do not have to talk about them in order. It is usually a good idea, however, because the points help you to organise what you are going to say.

IELTS Speaking Exam: Part 2

1 Read the Part 2 task card and the notes that one candidate made for the questions. Notice that the candidate has not used full sentences. For example, instead of writing *It was a final so the atmosphere was electric*, he has written *final so atmosph. electric*. When we make notes, we often omit less important words such as articles and auxiliary verbs, and we often write only the key words. We also use shorthand, such as + for *and*, w. for *with*, and *yrs* for *years*. Develop your own shorthand in English as this will save you time.

Describe an exciting competition or sporting event you have witnessed.

You should say:

what the competition or sporting event was

when and where it took place

who won

and explain why it was exciting.

Past tenses! Don't sound bored!!!
What? tennis match, final
Where, when? outside Bdx, 6 yrs ago
Who won? M. won 2–1 (leave till end)
Why exciting? final so atmosph. electric,
close to action, loser expected to win but fell apart
Vocab – court, crowd, hit balls down the line, serve for the match, be presented w. the trophy

Now answer questions a–d.

a Which tenses will the candidate use? Why?
b Why do you think he has written *Don't sound bored*?
c Is he going to follow the order of the points on the card?
d Why do you think he has noted down vocabulary? Has he written just isolated words?

Give yourself one minute to plan your answer to the Part 2 Exam question using the ideas in Exercise 1. Whenever you practise Part 2 questions, always give yourself one minute, but no more, so that you learn how best to use the time. Then talk for one to two minutes.

3 Studies & work

Vocabulary: Studies and work

1   Read the information card below about a man called Mubarak. The card contains useful vocabulary for talking about studies and work so look up any words you do not know in a dictionary.

Name:	Mubarak
Nationality:	Emirati
Favourite subject at school:	Maths (likes using logic to work answers out)
Bachelor's and Master's degrees in:	Mechanical Engineering from Leeds University (more practical than Maths; wanted British qualifications)
Dream job:	Mechanical Engineer for UAE Army (good job security; high prestige; interesting)

2   Using the notes in Exercise 1, talk about Mubarak.

   Example: Mubarak is from the United Arab Emirates. At school, his favourite subject was Maths because ...

 3   Listen to Mubarak talking about his studies and dream job. He uses some useful vocabulary.

15
CD1

Listen again and write the words and phrases which correspond to definitions 1–11.

1 subjects such as history, literature, or languages in contrast to scientific subjects

_____

2 the examinations that you have passed after completing a course _____

3 the amount of money that you pay to a university for your education _____

4 talks that someone gives in order to teach people about a particular subject, usually at a university or college _____

5 classes at a college or university in which the teacher and a small group of students discuss a topic _____

6 I was unsuccessful in an exam _____

7 take an exam again because you did not pass it the first time _____

8 I was of an acceptable standard (in an exam) _____

9 work done by a student during their studies that forms part of their final grade or mark _____

10 my perfect job _____

11 a feeling of being safe and free from worry because your job is permanent

_____

4 Complete the passage about Julia with the words and phrases a–i, and the passage about Peter with the words and phrases j–s.

a	an office job	**d**	long hours	**g**	retired
b	earn	**e**	own boss	**h**	sacked
c	job satisfaction	**f**	redundant	**i**	self-employed

Julia: I'm (1) _____. I give art classes, mainly to (2) _____ people. I may not (3) _____ a great deal but I get an immense amount of (4) _____ because I see people who have barely held a brush before gain in confidence and learn new skills. I don't think I could cope with having (5) _____ – the monotony would drive me mad. People in offices seem to work (6) _____, and there's always the risk of being made (7) _____ or getting (8) _____. Nobody can fire me because I'm my (9) _____!

j	breadwinner	**n**	part-time	**q**	volunteer work
k	career-minded	**o**	responsible	**r**	wage
l	get home late	**p**	stay-at-home mum	**s**	workaholic
m	overtime				

Peter: I'm a water engineer. In my current job, I'm (10) _____ for designing flood defence systems and monitoring flood levels. I must admit that I'm a bit of a(n) (11) _____. I'm constantly doing (12) _____ – unpaid, I should add – and so I generally (13) _____. I would definitely say I live to work, not work to live. Years ago, I did a lot of (14) _____, advising people in developing countries on installing water supplies. However, since I've now settled down and am the main (15) _____, I feel I have to earn a decent (16) _____. My wife works (17) _____ but she only went back to work last month. Before that, she was a(n) (18) _____. I think she enjoyed looking after the kids but she's always been quite (19) _____ so she didn't want to stay a housewife forever.

5 **Complete sentences 1–10 with the correct form of the word in brackets.**

1 _____ is on the rise again. The queues outside the job centre just get longer and longer. (employ)

2 I have to make a _____ in front of about 200 people tomorrow. I'm so nervous. (present)

3 I think I'm due for a _____ soon because I've been in my current role for nearly four years now and I always get good feedback. (promote)

4 We have _____ every six months, where we discuss with our boss how we've been doing and set our goals for the next six months. (appraise)

5 Vast numbers of workers are being _____ at the moment – business is not what it used to be. (lay off)

6 I fear finding staff with adequate levels of experience may prove _____. (problem)

7 My _____ include filing and answering the phone. (responsible)

8 Teaching is apparently one of the most _____ jobs there is. And, if I think how naughty my friends and I used to be at school, I'm not surprised! (stress)

9 I work in a bank so I'm used to _____ with customers. (deal)

10 My colleague was given the job of team leader, which is strange as she is by far the most _____ member of staff. She's only nineteen, after all. (experience)

IELTS Speaking Exam: Part 1

6 You are going to hear questions that are typical of Part 1 of the exam. Listen to each question and give your answer. Record your answers.

Now listen to the sample answer and note down any useful words and phrases.

16
CD1

IELTS Speaking Exam: Part 2

7 Read this Part 2 question. Give yourself one minute to plan your answer, making notes if you wish. Then talk for one to two minutes.

> Describe your dream job.
>
> You should say:
>
> > what qualifications or experience you would need
> >
> > what the job would involve
> >
> > what you think the most difficult thing about the job would be
>
> and explain why it is your dream job.

Grammar: Speculating

The questions above ask about an unreal situation. To talk about an unreal situation, you can use *would* + infinitive.

Example: My dream job would be to teach children to sail.

You probably do not know about every aspect of your dream job. For example, you may not know exactly what the job would involve. If this is the case, you will have to speculate.

8 Listen to the sample answer and then read Track 17, page 103. Underline the language the candidate uses to speculate about the job.

Example: I imagine the job would involve ...

Here is some useful language for speculating:

maybe, perhaps: *Perhaps the job is more difficult than it seems.*

It is fairly/quite/very/extremely (un)likely (that) ...: *It is fairly likely I would need more qualifications. It is extremely unlikely that I would ever get such a job.*

I'd hazard a guess (that) ...: *I'm not sure, but I'd hazard a guess that it's not as well paid as being an accountant.*

It is quite possible (that) ...: *It is quite possible that managers often wish they didn't have so much responsibility.*

I imagine/suspect (that) ...: *I suspect that I wouldn't find it a very satisfying role.*

You can also use modals to speculate:

must + infinitive: *Being a miner must be a dangerous job.*
(You are guessing, but you are almost certain it is dangerous.)

can't + infinitive: *It can't be very rewarding.*
(You are guessing, but you are almost certain it is <u>not</u> rewarding.)

9 Speculate about jobs 1–8 using the language on page 27. Think about work hours (how long and what part of the day they work), how much job satisfaction they have, what their job involves, etc.

Examples: Being a politician must be difficult because there's always somebody who disagrees with you.
I'd hazard a guess that a chef works longer hours than a clown.

1 a politician   **4** a chef   **7** a soldier
2 a university lecturer   **5** a musician   **8** an office junior
3 a clown   **6** an astronaut

10 What is the difference in meaning between the three conditionals?

1 **First conditional:** *If I study harder, I will get my dream job.*
if + present tense, *will/can/may/might/could/be going to* + infinitive OR
will/can/may/might/could/be going to + infinitive + *if* + present tense

2 **Second conditional:** *If I studied harder, I would get my dream job.*
if + past tense, *would/might/could* + infinitive OR
would/might/could + infinitive + *if* + past tense

3 **Third conditional:** *If I had studied harder, I would have got my dream job.*
if + past perfect, *would/might/could have* + past participle OR
would/might/could have + past participle + *if* + past perfect

Note: We use mixed conditionals when the time of the *if* clause is not the same as the time of the result clause.

If you had taken that job (in the past), *you would be a manager now.*

If she were a dentist (in the present), *she would have got a job in the UK* (in the past).

11 Rewrite sentences 1–4 using the alternatives to *if* in brackets.

1 I'll get into university if I get straight As. (provided that)

_____

2 If my CV doesn't stand out, I will never be called for an interview. (unless)

_____

3 If I pass my final exams, I've got a chance of getting my dream job. (as long as)

_____

4 I will never be an athlete, even if I train really hard. (no matter how)

_____

12 Answer the Part 2 Exam question in Exercise 7 again, but this time include some of the language for speculation and conditional constructions you have learnt.

18
CD1

IELTS Speaking Exam: Part 3

13 You are going to hear questions that are typical of Part 3 of the exam. Listen to each question and record your answers.

Now listen to the sample answer. What additional vocabulary could you use in your own answers?

Pronunciation: Word stress

14 Underline the syllable that is stressed in words 1–4. Check your answers in a dictionary.

1 leader   2 hotel   3 production   4 desert (*verb*)

19
CD1

Now listen to the words and practise pronouncing them correctly. The stressed syllable is generally louder and longer.

> **Exam tip:** Something the examiner will be thinking about as you talk is, 'Does this student impose a strain on the listener?' This is a very important concept in the IELTS Speaking exam. If you 'impose a strain', it means that the listener has to struggle to understand you.
>
> Here are some ways you may impose a strain:
>
> • hesitating for too long
> • speaking too quietly
> • having poor pronunciation
>
> Improving these aspects of your speaking will improve your mark.
>
> Word stress is crucial in English. If you stress the wrong syllable, the listener may have trouble understanding you. Always mark the stressed syllable when you note down a new word.

15 There are some rules for word stress in English, although there are also many exceptions to the rules. Read the following rules and answer the questions.

Rule a: Two-syllable nouns and adjectives are most often stressed on the first syllable.

1 Which word from Exercise 14 follows this rule? Can you think of three more?

2 Which word from Exercise 14 is an exception to this rule? Can you think of any other exceptions?

Rule b: There are words that can be either a noun or a verb. If they are spelt the same and have two syllables, the noun (and adjective) is usually stressed on the first syllable, whereas the verb on the second syllable.

3 Which word from Exercise 14 follows this rule? Do you know any other words that follow the rule?

Rule c: Words that end in *-sion* and *-tion* have the stress on the penultimate (next to last) syllable.

4 Which word from Exercise 14 follows this rule? Try to think of three others.

16 The words in italics in sentences 1–7 follow rule b in Exercise 15 above. Decide if the words are nouns, adjectives or verbs and underline the stressed syllable. Then practise pronouncing them correctly in the sentences.

1 He *presented* me with my degree certificate.

2 I *object* to being treated like that. I'm going to resign.

3 I *suspect* you mainly focus on your impending retirement.

4 This can lead to an *increase* in motivation.

5 They can *progress* steadily ...

6 Has the *transfer* taken place?

7 My family have an *export* business.

17 Check that you know the meanings of the words below. Then put them in the correct column, 1–4 below, according to their stress pattern.

prestigious   frustrating   fundamental   security
interesting   experience   redundant   difficult
responsible   seminar   lecturer   consider
motivate   foreigner   entertaining   workaholic

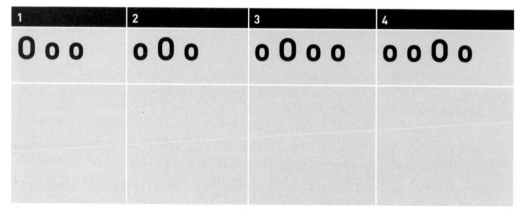

1	2	3	4
O o o	o O o	o O o o	o o O o

20
CD1

Listen and check your answers. Use a dictionary if you are still not sure which syllables are stressed.

Now practise saying the words. Test yourself by writing the words on cards and trying to remember the correct pronunciation.

18 Listen to your recorded answer to the Part 3 questions in Exercise 13.

Did you use any of the words from Exercise 16 or 17? If so, did you pronounce them correctly?

Write down ten words you used in your answer that you want to check the pronunciation of. Where is the main stress in these words? Practise saying them in isolation.

Answer the Part 3 questions again, this time paying attention to the pronunciation of these words.

Exam technique: Giving answers that are the right length

1   Below are some possible answers to the Part 1 questions you heard in Exercise 13.
For each question, decide which you think is the best. Give reasons why the other answers
are less satisfactory.

Note: the English is correct in all the answers.

1   Do you work or are you a student?

    a   I work.

    b   I'm currently studying history at Moscow State University. I'm in my second year.

    c   I work as a dentist in Budapest. It's a very rewarding job and I earn good money. We
get vast numbers of foreigners coming to get dental treatment in Hungary because
it's far cheaper here than in many other countries. As well as being cheap, we offer
high quality dental care and our patients are always happy with our work. I had to
study for many years to be a dentist but it was worth it. People generally respect
you for being a dentist as it's considered to be a good job, although perhaps it isn't
as prestigious as being a doctor. I could have chosen to be a doctor and in fact, this
is what my father wanted me to do. However, I have some friends who are doctors
and they say they work very long hours and can't spend enough time with their
families. I think I made the right career choice.

2   Why did you choose that course or job?

    a   I didn't choose it.

    b   I chose it because French was always my best subject at school and I enjoy meeting
new people. I thought interpreting would suit me, therefore, as you have to be a
good communicator and of course skilled in foreign languages.

3   What is the most difficult thing about your studies or job?

    a   I'm not sure. Er ... I would say the most difficult thing is that we have tight deadlines,
so I'll be given a project and then told it's to be completed in one week, which is
nowhere near enough time. That's difficult but it doesn't stop me enjoying my work.

    b   I don't enjoy attending meetings. It's often very boring and the meetings last too
long.

2   Play the Part 1 questions and sample answers on Track 16 again. Then answer the
questions yourself but this time, try to make sure your answers are relevant and of an
appropriate length.

16
CD1

4   The world around us

Vocabulary: The environment

1   Complete sentences 1–7 with words a–g. The sentences are all about ways to help the environment.

a	Boycott	**c**	Recycle	**e**	Switch	**g**	Walk
b	Buy	**d**	Reduce	**f**	Use		

1   _____ paper, cans, plastic, glass and other items like mobiles.

2   _____ less water in the house and garden.

3   _____ the amount of household waste you produce.

4   _____ to energy efficient light bulbs.

5   _____ products that harm the environment, such as those made from mahogany, which grows in rainforests.

6   _____, cycle or use public transport instead of driving your car.

7   _____ organic foods that do not use harmful artificial fertilisers and pesticides.

2 Now think about these questions:

Which of the things 1–7 in Exercise 1 do you do?
Do you do anything else to help the environment?

Practise talking about what you do for the environment and give details. If you do not do any of the things 1–7, say which ideas you think sound the most effective and why. Here are some useful phrases:

In our household, we . . .
I try to reduce my carbon footprint by . . . (-ing)
I think . . . (-ing) sounds like the best idea.

Vocabulary: Climate

21
CD1

3 Listen to the speakers 1–3 talking about their countries' climates. Which country is each speaker talking about? Write *Wales, Saudi Arabia* or *Iceland*. If you need to, read Track 21 on page 105.

Speaker 1 _____
Speaker 2 _____
Speaker 3 _____

4 Find words and expressions in Track 21, page 105, associated with hot, cold, wet and dry climates and write them in the table below.

Hot climate	Cold climate	Wet climate	Dry climate

5 Complete the texts below with words a–j, which collocate with the words in italics.

a	biting	**e**	high	**h**	flooding
b	bitterly	**f**	boiling	**i**	rain
c	hot	**g**	rainy	**j**	unbearable
d	heavy				

In my country, we have a (1) _____ *season*. During this time, there is really (2) _____ *humidity* so it gets awfully (3) _____ *and sticky*, and we often get (4) *torrential* _____, which can cause (5) *severe* _____. In the early summer, before the rains come, it tends to be (6) _____ *hot*. Most tourists (7) *find the heat* _____, actually, so I wouldn't recommend visiting then.

In the winter, it gets (8) _____ *cold*. We get (9) _____ *winds*, so cold that I have heard of people's ears freezing and then snapping off! Not only that but we get such (10) _____ *snow* that some people's houses get completely covered by snowdrifts and they have to be dug out.

6 Match sentences 1–8 to people a–c.

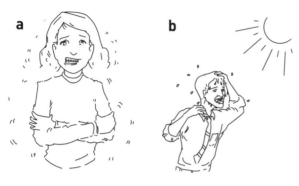

1 I'm soaked to the skin. _____

2 I feel so dehydrated. _____

3 I wish I had my waterproofs on. _____

4 I'm drenched. _____

5 My teeth are chattering. _____

6 I wish I was wearing more layers. _____

7 I'm frozen to the bone. _____

8 I wish I could find some shade. _____

7 *Get* is one of the most common verbs in English. It has many meanings.

*Examples: We often **get** thick fog. (get = have)*
   *In the winter, it **gets** absolutely freezing. (gets = becomes)*
   *The temperature often **gets** above 40°C. (gets = reaches)*

Tends to be is another useful phrase for talking about the weather.

*Example: In the summer, it **tends to be** hot. (tends to be = is usually)*

Complete the sentences to describe the seasons in your country or region.

Examples: In the spring, we sometimes get quite mild weather.
   In the rainy season, it tends to be very hot and sticky.

In _____ we (sometimes/often/always) get _____.

In _____ it (sometimes/often/always) gets _____.

In _____ the temperature (sometimes/often/always) gets _____.

In _____ it tends to be _____.

IELTS Speaking Exam: Part 1

8 You are going to hear questions that are typical of Part 1 of the exam. Listen to each question and give your answer using language from Exercise 5. Record your answers.

22
CD1

Grammar: Cleft sentences

We use cleft sentences to emphasise information we particularly want to focus on, perhaps because the information is new or surprising, because it offers a contrast with what someone else has said, or because we are expressing a strong preference or attitude.

The typical structure of an *it*-cleft sentence is: *it + be + emphasised information + relative clause.*

Simple sentence:	*Torrential rain is the main cause of flooding.*
Cleft sentence:	*It is torrential rain that is the main cause of flooding.*

The typical structure of a *what*-cleft sentence is: *what-clause + be + emphasised information.*

Simple sentence:	*We like to spend our summers by the lake.*
Cleft sentence:	*What we like is to spend our summers by the lake.*

9 **1** Rewrite the simple sentence below as an *it*-cleft sentence.
Simple sentence: *I can't stand the monsoon season.*
Cleft sentence: _____

2 Rewrite the simple sentence below as a *what*-cleft sentence.
Simple sentence: *I want to go to the beach.*
Cleft sentence: _____

10 Listen to the sample answers to the Part 1 questions in Exercise 7. Then read the Track 23, page 105 and underline three cleft sentences.
23
CD1

11 There are other kinds of cleft structures too. Complete sentences 1–3 so they are true for you. Then rewrite them as cleft sentences using the structures given.

1 I (dis)like warm weather because _____.
The reason why _____.
2 I spend my summers in/at _____.
The place where _____.
3 I dislike _____ weather most of all because _____.
The weather that _____.

> **Exam tip:** You can use cleft sentences to answer questions the examiner asks you. For example:
>
> **Examiner:** What do you do when it's cold outside?
> **Candidate:** What we tend to do is stay in and watch our favourite films.
>
> **Examiner:** Which season is your favourite?
> **Candidate:** Well, what I like best are the transitions between the seasons, when you first feel the weather begin to change.

Grammar: Complex sentences

IELTS Speaking Exam: Part 2

12 Read this Part 2 question and think about how you might answer it.

> Describe your favourite season.
>
> You should say:
>> what the season is and when it occurs
>>
>> what the weather is like during this season
>>
>> what your typical activities are during this season
>
> and explain why it is your favourite season.

It would be easy to answer this question using only simple sentences. For example:

Most people prefer the summer. My favourite season is spring. It is not too hot. I often go for long walks.

However, you will not achieve a high score if you use only simple sentences like this.

1 We can join the first two sentences using *although*.

Although most people prefer the summer, my favourite season is spring. OR

My favourite season is spring although most people prefer the summer.

2 We can join the last two sentences using *since* (as a conjunction meaning *because*).

Since it is not too hot, I often go for long walks. OR

I often go for long walks since it is not too hot.

13 1 Join these two sentences using *although*.

Snow is beautiful to look at. It makes it difficult to get to work.

_____

2 Join these two sentences using *since* (as a conjunction meaning *because*).

It rains so much in my country. We spend a lot of our time indoors.

_____

Grammar: Subordinate clauses

A subordinate clause is a clause that cannot be a complete sentence in itself. It must be joined to a main clause, which can be a complete sentence in itself.

The typical structure of a complex sentence with a subordinate clause is:

subordinate clause + adverbial subordinating conjunction + main clause OR
main clause + adverbial subordinating conjunction + subordinate clause

Example: Whereas I like hot weather, my sister likes cold weather.
My sister likes cold weather whereas I like hot weather.

Note: Most adverbial subordinating conjunctions, including those in these exercises, and their clauses can go at the beginning or the end of a sentence.

14 Complete sentences 1–7 using your own ideas. The words in italics are adverbial subordinating conjunctions.

1 *Although* it was windy, _____.
2 _____ *while* the snow was falling.
3 *Because* I want to help to protect the environment, _____.
4 *Whenever* the sun shines, _____.
5 *Whatever* the weather, _____.
6 *Rather than* driving to work, _____.
7 _____ *as soon as* it stops raining.

15 Give yourself one minute to plan your answer to the Part 2 question in Exercise 12, making notes if you wish. Then talk for one to two minutes. Use one or two cleft sentences, and one or two sentences with subordinating conjunctions in your answer.

🎧 24 CD1 **16** Listen to the sample answer to the Part 2 question in Exercise 12. Find some useful language to use in your own answers.

Pronunciation: Long and short vowel sounds

🎧 25 CD1 **17** There are five long vowel sounds in English. Listen to the sounds and the words with these sounds. Then listen again and repeat.

1 /ɑː/ bard
2 /iː/ bead
3 /ɜː/ bird
4 /ɔː/ board
5 /uː/ booed

🎧 26 CD1 **18** There are seven short vowel sounds. Here you have six of them; the other is the schwa, /ə/, which you will study in later units. Listen to the sounds and the words with these sounds. Then listen again and repeat.

1 /æ/ pat
2 /e/ pet
3 /ɪ/ pit
4 /ɒ/ pot
5 /ʊ/ put
6 /ʌ/ putt

🎧 27 CD1 **19** You may find it difficult to pronounce words with short and long vowel sounds distinctly. For example, do you pronounce *sleep* (long vowel) the same as *slip* (short vowel)? Listen to the pairs of words on Track 27, where the only difference is the vowel sound. Then listen again and repeat, trying to pronounce the words accurately.

Short vowels		Long vowels	
1 /ɒ/	shot	/ɔː/	short
2 /ɒ/	cot	/ɔː/	caught
3 /ɪ/	slip	/iː/	sleep
4 /ɪ/	hill	/iː/	heel
5 /ʊ/	pull	/uː/	pool
6 /ʊ/	look	/uː/	Luke

20 Read the pairs of words 1–4. Then listen and underline the word you hear.

1	skid	2	pitch	3	full	4	wok
	skied		peach		fool		walk

Work with an English-speaking friend. Say one of the words from each pair above. Your friend must guess whether it is a word with a long or short vowel sound. Then swap roles.

21 English spelling is far from phonetic, but certain letters are often used to represent certain sounds, and this can help you to guess whether a word has a long or short vowel sound. Look at the table below. Add at least one more example word for each vowel spelling.

Vowel sounds	Common spellings	Example words
/ɪ/	i	igloo _____
/iː/	ee	tree _____
	ea	beach _____
	e	he _____
/æ/	a	bat _____
/ɑː/	ar	far _____
	a	plant _____
/ɒ/	o	dog _____
/ɔː/	or	tortoise _____
	a	fall _____
	aw	paw _____

Vowel sounds	Common spellings	Example words
/ʌ/	u	sun _____
/e/	e	nest _____
/ɜː/	er	person _____
	ir	girl _____
	ur	hurt _____
/uː/	oo	moon _____
	u	computer _____
/ʊ/	u	put _____
	oo	foot _____
	ou	could _____

Exam tip: In the IELTS Speaking exam, the examiner will listen for accurate pronunciation of short and long vowel sounds.

Which vowel sounds do you find it difficult to pronounce, maybe because they do not exist in your language? Find words with these sounds, find a 'talking' dictionary (electronic or online) so you can hear the words being pronounced, and practise saying them.

Which vowel sounds do you find it difficult to differentiate? Find minimal pairs, where the only difference between two words is the vowel sound. You can find examples of minimal pairs online or in pronunciation books. Practise pronouncing the minimal pairs accurately.

22 Ask an English-speaking friend to listen to your recorded answer to the Part 2 questions in Exercise 12. What do they think of your pronunciation of vowel sounds? Are any of your vowel sounds unclear or inaccurate? Practise those sounds and then re-record your answer, focusing on your pronunciation.

Exam technique: Using news articles to improve your answers

> **Exam tip:** The Part 3 topics do not require specialist knowledge and you will not be marked on your opinions. However, you may find it difficult to think of enough to say and your answers may lack depth. For this reason, you should regularly read news articles to build up an awareness of current affairs and develop your opinions on a wide range of topics, such as the ones in this book.

1 Read the following excerpt from a newspaper article.

What do you think about the article? Do you find the report worrying? What is your country doing to reduce its footprint? What are the environmental consequences of the lifestyles that the people in your country lead?

Do some research, make some notes, and then discuss the topic with someone. How do your views differ?

We Will Need A Second Earth

A new report reveals that if we fail to reduce our rates of consumption, we will soon need a new earth to meet our needs. The report, issued by conservation groups, warns that our demands on natural resources are unsustainable and that if they continue to rise at the same rate, by the mid-2030s we will require a second planet to maintain our lifestyles.

A spokesperson for one group said, 'Our reckless consumption is destroying the planet. In addition, there are economic repercussions - with the unprecedented depletion of natural resources, food, water and energy costs are set to soar.' The US and China are the worst offenders, together accounting for forty per cent of the global ecological footprint.

IELTS Speaking Exam: Part 3

2 You are now going to hear some Part 3 questions. The research you have done, and your practice discussing the topic, should mean that you have much to say. Pause the CD after each question and give your answer.

Now listen to the sample answer and read Track 29 on page 106.

29
CD1

5 Communication

Aims: Talking about languages, keeping in touch, globalisation

Making comparisons | Expressing attitude | Pronunciation: Consonants

Exam technique: Giving yourself time to think

Vocabulary: Languages

30 CD1 🎧 **1** Listen to someone talking about the languages they speak. Listen again and write the words and phrases that correspond to definitions 1–6. You will hear the answers in order.

1 the language that you learn from your parents when you are a baby _____

2 able to speak more than two languages very well _____

3 able to speak the language easily and correctly _____

4 speak a language well enough to communicate about basic things _____

5 not as good at something as you used to be because you have not done it for a long time _____

6 learn something without effort over a period of time _____

Listen again and find five collocations with the word *language* that correspond to definitions 7–11.

7 a language that is spoken internationally _____

8 a language that is spoken by only a small proportion of people in a country _____

9 a language that is not spoken as a native language in your country _____

10 a language that is used by many people _____

11 a language that you speak well but that is not your native language _____

2   Complete sentences 1–4 with words a–e.

   a accents   **c** dubbed   **e** subtitled

   b dialects   **d** loanwords

1 British and American English are different _____ of English – there are some differences in vocabulary and grammar.

2 When they are shown in cinemas in my country, American films tend to be _____. I wish they were _____ instead because then I could improve my English while I watch.

3 French has a lot of _____ from English, for example *week-end*, *job*, and *jeans*.

4 My friends and I speak with northern _____.

Vocabulary: Keeping in touch

3   Look at the phrases with *touch* and their meanings. Then complete sentences 1–3 with the correct form of the phrases.

keep in touch: write to, phone, or visit someone regularly

lose touch: gradually stop writing to, telephoning, or visiting someone

get back in touch: communicate with someone again after not communicating with them for a while

1 I _____ with my old colleagues since leaving my last job, but then we were never very close.

2 He still _____ with Rose although they haven't seen each other in years.

3 I asked John for Mel's new number because I wanted _____ with her.

4   You can keep in touch with people: by phone, by letter, by text message, by email, via social networking sites, like Facebook. Or you can meet face-to-face. For example, you can: meet up for coffee, go out together (e.g. to a club or the cinema or a restaurant), go round to each other's houses.

How do you keep in touch with people you know? Do you keep in touch with different people in different ways? Practise giving your answers and your reasons.

Vocabulary: Globalisation

5   Read the text below and correct the words in italics by using another form of the word.

The (1) *integrate* _____ of the world's economies and cultures is (2) *common* _____ known as globalisation. Although there is nothing new about countries (3) *work* _____ closely together, globalisation is now happening at a (4) *remarked* _____ pace. This is (5) *large* _____ due to (6) *technology* _____ advances. Television channels such as the BBC are available throughout the world, and many clothing and food brands are (7) *recognised* _____ to people of almost any nationality. In addition, the Internet (8) *create* _____ a common (9) *globe* _____ culture, one which is predominantly English (10) *speaker* _____.

IELTS Speaking Exam: Part 1

6 You are going to hear questions that are typical of Part 1 of the exam. Listen to each question and give your answers using some of the vocabulary you have learnt so far in this unit. Record your answers.

Now listen to the sample answers. (See also Track 31, page 108.)

Grammar: Making comparisons

Imagine the following situation:

Mark got a band score of 3.5 in his IELTS exam. Anna got a band score of 6.5. Anita got a band score of 7.0.

We can use the comparative and superlative forms to compare their scores:

Anna got a higher score than Mark. (comparative)

Anita got the highest score (in the group). (superlative)

Look at the comparative and superlative forms outlined in the table below.

Adjectives	Comparative	Superlative
one-syllable adjectives e.g. *slow*	adjective + -er/r e.g. *slower*	the + adjective + -est/st e.g. *the slowest*
two-syllable adjectives ending in -y e.g. *easy*	adjective + -ier (*y* + -ier) e.g. *easier*	adjective + -iest (*y* + -iest) e.g. *the easiest*
two-syllable adjectives not ending in -y (1) e.g. *quiet*	adjective + -er e.g. *quieter*	the + adjective + -est/st e.g. *the quietest*
two-syllable adjectives not ending in -y (2) e.g. *modern*	*more* + adjective e.g. *more modern*	*the most* + adjective e.g. *the most modern*
two-syllable adjectives not ending in -y (3) e.g. *common*	adjective + -er/r OR *more* + adjective e.g. *commoner / more common*	*the* + adjective + -est/st OR *the most* + adjective e.g. *the commonest / the most common*
adjectives with more than two syllables e.g. *convenient*	*more* + adjective e.g. *more convenient*	*the most* + adjective e.g. *the most convenient*
irregular adjectives *good* *bad*	*better* *worse*	*the best* *the worst*

The opposite of *more* is *less*, and the opposite of *the most* is *the least*. However, note that we often avoid using *less*. Instead we use *not as ... as ...* or an opposite adjective, especially with one-syllable adjectives.

Example: a high score → a lower score (not *a less high score*).

7 **Make six sentences comparing the ways of keeping in touch and meeting from Exercise 4. Use comparative or superlative forms of the adjectives below or other adjectives.**

bad	convenient	easy	fast	good
impersonal	modern	old-fashioned	personal	slow

Example: Using a social networking site may be easier than meeting face-to-face, but it is also less personal.

8 We can use words like *much* and *a bit* in comparative sentences to modify the adjective:

much (= a lot): *Texting is **much** quicker than writing a letter.*
a bit (= a little): *Texting is **a bit** quicker than emailing.*

We can also use words like *significantly*, *slightly*, *marginally* and *far*. Which words have a similar meaning to *much*? Which have a similar meaning to *a bit*?

We can also use certain words in superlative sentences to modify the adjective:
by far (= by a great amount): *American films are **by far** the most popular films in my country.*
easily (= without question): *Toni is **easily** the best student in our class.*

Modify the sentences you wrote in Exercise 7.2 using some of the words above.

*Example: Using a social networking site may be **much** easier than meeting face-to-face, but it is also **significantly** less personal.*

9 We can use the following structure to say that two things change together:

the + comparative (+ subject + verb), *the* + comparative (+ subject + verb)

Examples: The more languages you speak, the easier it is to learn a new one.

The sooner, the better.

1 Which word gives each sentence the correct meaning?

    a The *fewer/more* mistakes you make in the exam, the better score you get.

    b The more you practise speaking the *less/more* fluent you will become.

2 Make sentences that describe how you think the things below change together.

    a languages you speak, your earning potential

    b the spread of English and the culture of English-speaking countries, local languages and traditions

10 We can express the idea that things are equal or not equal in several ways.

We use *as ... as ...* to say two things are equal in some way:
*Marie's accent is **as** difficult to understand **as** Sophie's.*
(= Marie's accent and Sophie's accents are equally difficult to understand.)

We use *nearly as ... as ...* to say two things are almost equal.
*My mum's English is nearly **as** good **as** mine.*
(= My English is better than my mum's, but only a little better.)

We use *not as ... as ...* to say two things are not equal in some way.
*Hungarian is **not as** widely spoken **as** English.*
(= Hungarian is less widely spoken than English.)

Write a total of six sentences with *as ... as ...*, *nearly as ... as ...*, **and** *not as ... as ...* **relating to your life.**

Expressing attitude

11 You can make your language more interesting by expressing your attitude with precision. One way to do this is with attitude markers. These are often adverbs, but they can also be phrases and they modify a whole sentence or clause. Their position in a sentence is generally very flexible.

*Example: British people **apparently** spend an average of £90 a month on communication services. They have increased their use of such services in recent years but, **interestingly**, they spend less money on them because competition between companies has reduced the charges.*

Check the meanings of the attitude markers a–g in your dictionary. Then use them to complete sentences 1–7. There is sometimes more than one possible answer.

a admittedly   **d** as luck would have it   **f** ideally

b all things considered   **e** even more importantly   **g** undoubtedly

c arguably

1 Due to the emergence of China as a leading economic power, Mandarin will _____ become the foreign language of choice in future years. I am sure of it.

2 _____, I'd like to study at a British university but I'm not sure I'll be able to. For financial reasons, I may have to stay here instead.

3 My friend wants to improve her speaking and, _____, our school has just set up an English conversation club.

4 _____, English is a more useful language to learn than Italian. I still prefer Italian, though.

5 _____, I could have got a better mark if I had spent more time studying and less time partying.

6 Pronunciation is _____ the most difficult aspect of speaking English.

7 To have a good grasp of English you must know about collocations. _____, you must practise speaking English and use those collocations as much as you can.

Here are some more attitude markers you can use in your speaking. There is an almost unlimited number of attitude markers, so look out for them when you read or listen to English.

definitely	(un)fortunately	inevitably	obviously
of course	predictably	sadly	strangely
(un)surprisingly	thank goodness	thankfully	undeniably

> **Exam tip:** As you learn new aspects of language, such as attitude markers, there are two important things to remember:
>
> **Learn them properly.** It is not enough to memorise lists of words. Look up the words and phrases in your dictionary, study example sentences, look for these words and phrases in context, and practise using the new vocabulary and structures.
>
> **Do not overuse them.** Using attitude markers in every sentence, for example, will make your English sound unnatural. Again, study the language in context to see how native speakers use them.

IELTS Speaking Exam: Part 2

12 Read this Part 2 question. Give yourself one minute to plan your answer, making notes if you wish. Think about how you could include some comparative structures as well as some attitude markers. Then record yourself speaking for one to two minutes.

> Describe a language other than English that you would like to learn.
>
> You should say:
>
> > what the language is
> >
> > where it is spoken
> >
> > what you think would be difficult and what would be easy about learning the language
>
> and explain why you would like to learn it.

13 Listen to the sample answer to the Part 2 question in Exercise 12. Then read Track 32, page 108 and underline the comparative structures and attitude markers.

32
CD1

Pronunciation: Consonants

 14

33
CD1

Listen to the consonants and the words with these consonants. Then listen again and repeat. Isolate the consonants you find difficult to pronounce, probably because they do not exist in your language or are pronounced slightly differently.

IPA: /p/ apart pop	IPA: /b/ by bob	IPA: /t/ tongue taste	IPA: /d/ do did	IPA: /tʃ/ mature church	IPA: /dʒ/ German judge	IPA: /k/ Korean clock	IPA: /g/ English gig
IPA: /f/ French tough	IPA: /v/ via revive	IPA: /θ/ think path	IPA: /ð/ this smooth	IPA: /s/ so success	IPA: /z/ easy zeros	IPA: /ʃ/ national Spanish	IPA: /ʒ/ television leisure
IPA: /m/ men mime	IPA: /n/ know nine	IPA: /ŋ/ sing language	IPA: /h/ hear perhaps	IPA: /l/ laugh lull	IPA: /r/ Russian rhetoric	IPA: /w/ whisper well	IPA: /j/ use few /fju/

1 The consonants in the first two rows of the chart form pairs (p/b; t/d; tʃ/dʒ; k/g; f/v; θ /dʒ; s/z; ʃ/ʒ): the only difference between them is that the first is unvoiced and the second is voiced. For example, you produce /p/ and /b/ in the same way, except that for /b/ your vocal chords vibrate.

2 Try saying the sounds with your hand on your throat. Can you feel the vibration? All the sounds in grey squares are voiced.

3 If you find a sound difficult, can you pronounce its partner? Remember the only difference is that one is unvoiced, the other voiced.

4 Find ten words containing the consonant(s) you find difficult to pronounce and practise saying them again and again. Record yourself. If your mother tongue has few final consonants, as in Thai or Mandarin, record yourself pronouncing words with consonants at the end, both alone and within sentences.

5 If you find it hard to differentiate two sounds, find minimal pairs, where the only difference between two words is those sounds, and practise pronouncing them accurately. For example, for /b/ versus /v/: *best/vest*, *jibe/jive*, *boat/vote*. Then ask a friend to listen as you say one word from each pair. Can they identify which word you are saying?

 15

34
CD1

If a word has a group of consonants with no vowels between them, it can be hard to pronounce. Listen and write the words you hear; they all contain consonant clusters. Then listen again and repeat. Make sure you do not add vowels before or between the consonant clusters.

IELTS Speaking Exam: Part 3

 16

35
CD1

Listen to the Part 3 questions. Answer them, aiming for accurate pronunciation of any difficult consonants or consonant clusters.

Now listen to the sample answers. (See also Track 35, page 109.)

Exam techniques: Giving yourself time to think

36
CD1

1 Listen to a candidate talking to the examiner during the exam. What language does she use to give herself time to think?

Now read Track 36 on page 110 and underline the language she uses.

> **Exam tip**: Although you should not overuse language such as *um* and *er*, using such language is not a sign of 'bad English'. All native speakers make use of these strategies.

2 You can also use whole phrases to give yourself time to think:

That's a tough question.

That's an interesting question.

It's very difficult to know for sure, but I think/perhaps/it's possible ...

Play Track 36 and listen to the examiner's question again. Respond using one of the phrases above.

37
CD1

3 Listen and underline the language the candidates use to contradict the examiner politely (see also Track 37, page 110).

To be polite, you must use polite language together with polite intonation. Listen again and imitate the speakers' intonation.

4 You may want to confirm what the examiner says. Read the exchanges below and underline the language the candidates use to do that.

Examiner: Are social networking sites the most popular way for young people to communicate with each other?

Candidate: Yes, they certainly are. It's no doubt because it is free and simple ...

Examiner: Are you saying that more and more people are texting to keep in touch?

Candidate: Precisely. It is fast becoming the most popular means of communication ...

6 Technology

Vocabulary: Technology

1   **Read the text and answer questions 1–7 below.**

> While technophiles love gadgets and all that is state-of-the-art believing that
> technology can solve all our problems, there are people who shrink in fear at the
> prospect of encountering cutting-edge technology. What is at the root of their
> panic? Well, technophobes are fixated on what could go wrong and allow their fears
> to completely dominate their view of any development in AI, genetic engineering
> or modern medicine. While we're busy upgrading our MP3 players to the latest
> model, they're hoping all this gadgetry will go away, clinging stubbornly to outdated
> equipment and trusty pen and paper.

1   Explain in your own words what a technophile is and what a technophobe is. Which are
     you? Which do people of your generation tend to be?

2   Is the writer of the text a technophile or a technophobe?

3   Give three examples of *gadgets*. Are you into gadgets?

4   The writer talks about *cutting-edge* technology. Find a synonym for *cutting-edge* in the
     text.

5   Find an antonym for *cutting-edge* in the text.

6   What does *AI* mean? Do you know of any recent developments in AI? What do you think
     is the future of AI?

7   Have you recently upgraded your mobile or your MP3 player? Why is it important to you
     (or to some people) to have the latest model?

2 Many phrasal verbs have more than one meaning. Complete each pair of sentences 1–6 below with the correct form of one of the phrasal verbs a–f. In the second sentence of each pair, the phrasal verb has a meaning connected with technology or science.

a	break down	**c**	turn down	**e**	set off
b	turn up	**d**	blow up	**f**	turn over

1a They _____ the bridge this morning so the enemy wouldn't be able to cross it.

1b They _____ the photo I took and made a poster out of it.

2a I'm afraid to report that talks between the two sides _____. It is therefore unlikely an agreement will be reached.

2b Your body _____ fat to create energy.

3a I waited for two hours but you didn't _____. Where were you?

3b Can you _____ the heating? I'm freezing.

4a The job did sound really interesting but I'm going to _____ it _____ because it would be too long a commute.

4b _____ the music _____. You'll make yourself deaf!

5a He _____ and went back to sleep.

5b This programme is so dull. Can we _____?

6a Have they left? Yes, they _____ at the crack of dawn.

6b The burglars _____ the alarm when they broke in, so that alerted the police.

3 Match each phrasal verb in the middle column to one meaning in column A and one meaning in column B.

A		B
(cause to) explode	**break down**	reduce the volume/temperature
reject	**turn down**	enlarge (a photo)
change position	**set off**	cause sth to operate
become ineffective	**turn up**	watch a different TV channel
start a journey	**blow up**	increase the volume/temperature
appear	**turn over**	separate into parts

Vocabulary: The Internet

4 How often do you use the Internet for the following activities?

chatting	shopping online	Internet dating	Internet gaming
social networking	reading online newspapers	research	learning
finding contact details	paying bills online	online banking	email

5 Match the dangers 1–4 to the descriptions a–d.

1 identity theft _____
2 viruses _____
3 cyber bullying _____
4 Internet addiction _____

   a when someone is harassed, threatened or humiliated over the Internet
   b when criminals steal your personal details and use them to get credit cards, passports, loans and so on
   c you need a firewall and antivirus software to protect your computer from these
   d excessive use of the computer that interferes with daily life

Now rate the dangers, 1 being the most worrying in your opinion, 4 the least worrying. Have you experienced any of them? With an English-speaking friend, discuss how you use the Internet and talk about its dangers. How do your habits, views and experiences differ?

IELTS Speaking Exam: Part 1

You are going to hear some questions that are typical of Part 1 of the exam. Listen to each question and give your answer. Try to use some of the vocabulary you have learnt so far in this unit.

Now listen to the sample answers.

38
CD1

Vocabulary: Phrasal verb particles

It can be difficult to guess the meaning of phrasal verbs and difficult to learn them. Learning about some general meanings of the particles will help you.

Particle	Meaning	Examples
up	increase	build up, grow up
down	decrease	calm down, cut down
	record in writing	write down, jot down
on	start	turn on, log on
	continue	carry on, stay on
off	end	ring off, turn off
	depart	set off, blast off
in	put into	plug in, stir in
	stay inside	stay in, lie in
out	be outside	go out, get out
away	avoid	keep away, look away

Note that there are more meanings for each particle, and also more particles. If you find this approach helpful, consult a book on phrasal verbs for more information.

7 Using the meanings outlined in the table on page 50, complete sentences 1–11 with the correct particle.

1 Can you log _____? I'd like to use the computer now.

2 Step _____ from the edge of the platform! It's dangerous.

3 Note this _____. You won't remember it otherwise.

4 We're going to eat _____ tonight. I might cook my speciality!

5 Slow _____. The speed limit's 30mph, not 40mph.

6 It's been lovely to see you, but I must rush _____ now or I'll be late.

7 They've failed twice already, but vow they're going to keep _____ trying.

8 If I read out the data will you key it _____?

9 Too much exercise can bring _____ an asthma attack.

10 I can't hear you. Please speak _____.

11 I've been locked _____ again. I've forgotten my keys and there's no one at home.

IELTS Speaking Exam: Part 2

8 **Read this example Part 2 question. Give yourself one minute to plan your answer, making notes if you wish. Then talk for one to two minutes and record your answer.**

Describe a piece of electronic equipment that you find useful.

You should say:

what the piece of equipment is

when and where you got it

what you use it for

and explain why you find it useful.

Note: *equipment* is uncountable, so do not say ~~an equipment~~ or ~~equipments~~. If you want to count it, use another noun: *a piece of equipment*. If you want to refer to it in a general sense, use the zero article: for example, *Equipment like this is indispensable.*

Listen to the sample answer. What phrase does the candidate use to introduce the talk?

_____

Pronunciation: Sentence stress

> **Exam tip:** Sentence stress gives English its rhythm. When a native speaker speaks English, they do not pronounce all words with equal stress. Important words are stressed and less important words are unstressed and are fitted in the spaces between the stressed words.

9 Look at the following chant and then listen to a native speaker saying it, pronouncing the stressed and unstressed (weak) words.

ONE		**TWO**		**THREE**		**FOUR**
ONE	and	**TWO**	and	**THREE**	and	**FOUR**
ONE	and then	**TWO**	and then	**THREE**	and then	**FOUR**
ONE	and then a	**TWO**	and then a	**THREE**	and then a	**FOUR**

Now try it for yourself. Say *one, two, three, four* as you clap. Then, without slowing down the clapping, add the word *and* between the claps. Then add *and then*, and then add *and then a*.

10 It is much easier to make *and then a* fit in the small spaces between the numbers if you use weak forms of the function words *and* and *a*. Listen and copy how the words are pronounced:

and /ən/   and then /ənðen/   and then a /ənðenə/

Listen and then say the chant again, using the weak forms. Try to speed up. Can you say it as quickly as the native speaker?

> **Exam tip:** Understanding and correctly using sentence stress will make a significant difference to your speaking. It will improve your fluency – you can speak more quickly and easily if you stress important words and do not stress less important words. It will also make your pronunciation closer to a native speaker's, and therefore easier for the examiner to understand without effort.

11 Look at the explanation and the table below.

In most neutral sentences, content words, which carry meaning, are stressed and function words, like prepositions, pronouns, and auxiliary verbs are unstressed.

Content words		Function words	
main verbs	*go, spoke, invented*	pronouns	*I, you, she, they*
nouns	*scientist, radio*	prepositions	*at, under, with*
adjectives	*interesting, clever*	articles	*a, the, some*
adverbs	*quickly, properly*	conjunctions	*and, but, so*
negative auxiliary verbs	*can't, don't, aren't*	auxiliary verbs	*can, should, must*
demonstratives	*this, that, these*	verb *be*	*is, am, was*
question words	*who, which, where*		

12
42
CD1

Listen to the recording and identify which words are stressed in sentences 1–4. Underline the stressed words.

1 It's a piece of equipment.

2 The latest trend is for green technology.

3 Do you know the price of this?

4 We can't speak English fluently. Can you?

Note that we sometimes stress function words, for example when they are at the end of a sentence, when a contrast is being expressed, or when the word is being said on its own.

In the four sentences above, only one function word is stressed. What is it and why is it stressed?

 13
43
CD1

The schwa /ə/ is the most common vowel sound in weak forms. It is also the most common vowel sound in the English language, occurring in many unstressed syllables.

1 Listen to it being pronounced. To say it, relax your mouth.

2 Listen to Track 42 again. Pay attention to how the function words are pronounced. Which function words contain a schwa?

Record yourself saying the sentences. Make sure you stress the content words and do not stress the 'weak' function words. Keep trying until you feel comfortable using sentence stress. Can you hear the improvement in your pronunciation?

3 Listen to your recording of your answer to Part 2 on page 51. Choose four sentences and write them down. Underline all the stressed syllables. Re-record the sentences stressing those syllables without stressing the rest.

 14
39
CD1

1 Play Track 39 again. Listen and try to hear the rhythms of the language, and the sentence stress.

2 Listen to the first sentence, pause the CD and repeat the sentence (using the transcript if you need to). Do the same for every sentence.

3 Then record yourself reading out the whole transcript until you feel confident in your use of sentence stress.

IELTS Speaking Exam: Part 3

 15
44
CD1

You are going to hear questions that are typical of Part 3 of the exam. Listen to each question and give your answer. Put into practice all you have learnt in this unit.

Now listen to the sample answers.

Exam technique: Coherence

1

1   Using your dictionary, check the meaning of *keyhole surgery*. Then reorder the sentences a–g.

    a   So, as you see, it really is a brilliant development.

    b   Then, surgeons can perform very delicate operations in this way.

    c   I believe keyhole surgery is one of the most significant developments in modern medicine.

    d   Last, but not least, recovery time is much quicker due again to the small incisions.

    e   There are numerous advantages.

    f   First of all, the surgeon can operate through tiny incisions so there is less scarring.

    g   It involves introducing a video camera into the body of a patient so the surgeon can watch what he is doing on a TV monitor.

    ———, ———, ———, ———, ———, ———, ———

2   Underline the language used to introduce each of the three advantages of keyhole surgery. You could also say *Firstly, Secondly, Thirdly/Lastly*.

3   What phrase is used to introduce the summary? Do you know any other phrases used for doing this?

45
CD1

2   Answer the question you hear, giving three advantages and a summarising statement using the language from Exercise 1.

46
CD1

3   This speaker gives two opposing ideas: one positive, the other negative. What phrase does she use to introduce the opposing idea?

47
CD1

4   Answer the question you hear by giving two opposing ideas. Link them using the phrase you have just learnt. What two phrases, involving the word *hand*, could you also use to give two opposing ideas?

5 Complete the lists of personal pronouns.

Subject pronouns	I	you	he	she	it	we	they
Object pronouns	me	___	___	___	___	___	___
Possessive pronouns	___	yours	___	___	X	___	___

6 Replace the words in italics in sentences a–d with pronouns.

a I asked if he wanted to borrow my phone because *his phone* had run out of battery.

b Scientists are often on the news, talking about their latest discoveries. I think *scientists* enjoy publicising what *scientists* do because all too often their work is ignored.

c Our invention was much more creative than *their invention*, but the judges awarded them the prize.

d I love video-calling my friends, but *video-calling my friends* can be embarrassing if I'm still in my pyjamas.

48
CD1

7 Be careful when using pronouns. Will the listener know what or who you are referring to? If it is not absolutely clear, repeat the noun instead. Listen to the recording. Is it clear who 'she' refers to?

8 In spoken English, if you do not know a person's gender or if it is not important, you can use pronouns. Replace the words in italics below with a pronoun.

If I met a genius scientist, my first question to *him or her* would definitely be why *he or she* hadn't come up with a cure for the common cold.

49
CD1

50
CD1

9 If, in the exam, you are talking about people from your country/region/city (including yourself) you can use *we*.

1 Listen and notice how the second version of the speech below sounds less repetitive.

2 Answer the question you hear, using *we* to describe people from your country including yourself.

> **Exam tip:** Make your speaking more coherent.
> - Use a range of methods – e.g. pronouns, 'signposting' phrases such as *first of all* and *so, as you see*, linking devices such as *although*.
> - Do not overuse any one phrase or method. This is worse than using no method at all because it will make your speech sound unnatural.
> - Ask a friend or teacher to listen to your recorded answers to some of the exam questions. Ask them to answer the following questions. Is your answer clear and easy to follow? If not, is it your ideas or your language that is confusing? Do you use a range of cohesive devices? Do you overuse any devices? Record your answer again, trying to make it clearer.

7 Hobbies

Vocabulary: Likes and dislikes

1 Look at statements a–g and decide if they express positive or negative feelings or
indifference about each activity.

   a I'm keen on photography. _____

   b I can't stand board games. _____

   c I'm crazy about computer games. _____

   d I don't mind cooking. _____

   e I'm fanatical about playing cards. _____

   f Going to the theatre? I can take it or
leave it. _____

   g Going to gigs is not my kind of thing.

      _____

2 Use each of the phrases in Exercise 1 to talk about how you feel about various pastimes.
There are some more pastimes you could talk about below. Practise saying your
sentences, paying attention to your pronunciation.

camping	crafts	eating out	fishing
entertaining	going clubbing	going for walks	listening to music
watching TV	woodwork	working on cars	

Vocabulary: Hobbies

3 **1** Complete each text with the words below. Words that form collocations are in italics.

1 Reading

about   character   opening   page-turner   set

The novel I'm reading at the moment is *a real* (1) _____. I just can't put it down. It's (2) _____ *in* Renaissance Italy and *is* (3) _____ young women who are forced to become nuns because they've brought shame on their families for various reasons. *In the* (4) _____ *chapters*, for example, a (5) _____ falls in love with her music teacher and the family don't approve.

2 Art

abstract   exhibition   hype   original   representational   work

I'm sorry to say the student *art* (1) _____ was rather dull. I had expected it to be really thought-provoking after *all the* (2) _____ but none of the art was very (3) _____. It was mostly sculpture, though there were a couple of installations and quite a few paintings. Most of the painters seemed to think they needed to be *strictly* (4) _____, but I prefer (5) _____ *art*. It allows you to respond more personally to a (6) _____ *of art*.

3 Music

charts   concert   gigs   live   lyrics   taken up   tunes

I've just (1) _____ *the piano*. It was after a (2) _____ I went to that inspired me because the pianist was so talented. I love (3) _____ *performances*, though usually I'm more into (4) _____. I went to see my favourite band the other week, actually. What I like about them is their *thoughtful* (5) _____ and *catchy* (6) _____. Of course, the band write their own music unlike the manufactured groups you see so much these days. They always *reach the top of the* (7) _____ but I think it's more down to marketing than talent.

4 Film

genre   predictable   rave   rom-com   slow-moving   star-studded

When it comes to film, my favourite (1) _____ is comedy. I went to see a (2) _____ last night, and it was so hilarious. It was well acted – well, it was a (3) _____ *cast* so that's not surprising. And it was so touching. Last weekend, my friends made me go and see a horror film with them. It was terrible, not scary at all. It was a (4) _____ *plot* and the ending was so (5) _____. My friends had wanted to see it for ages because it's getting (6) _____ *reviews* so they were really disappointed.

2 Check the meaning of any new vocabulary in these texts. Remember the correct definition may not be the first one in your dictionary. Note down any useful phrases, such as *I just can't put it down* and *they write their own music*.

Language: Frequency

4 1 The phrases below express frequency. Put them in order from the most frequent to the least frequent.

once a fortnight	every single day
every other day	several times a year
every Tuesday	twice a year

2 Practise talking about things you do and how often you do them. You can change some of the phrases above to make them true for you.

*Examples: I sing karaoke **every other Saturday**. I go to the theatre **about three times a year**.*

51
CD1

IELTS Speaking Exam: Part 1

5 You are going to hear Part 1 questions that are typical of the exam. Listen to each question and give your answer. Record yourself. Remember, do not give answers that are too short: saying just one word or one short sentence is not enough.

Now listen to the sample answers. Notice that the candidate uses a range of language to express likes and dislikes, and a range of frequency phrases.

IELTS Speaking Exam: Part 2

6 Read this Part 2 question. Give yourself one minute to plan your answer, making notes if you wish, then record yourself answering it. By now, you should be finding it easier to speak for two minutes on a topic.

> Describe a hobby you enjoy.
>
> You should say:
>
>> how long you have been doing it
>>
>> how often you do it
>>
>> what benefits you get from it
>
> and explain why you enjoy it.

Now listen to the sample answer.

Grammar: Present perfect

7 Read the rules and complete the example sentences.

We use the present perfect:

1 to talk about something that began in the past and continues now.
Complete the gaps with the present perfect and *for* with a period of time, and *since* with a point in time.

I _____ (live) in Granada _____ over ten years and have no plans to move. I love it here.

I _____ (know) her _____ before she was famous. She hasn't changed at all.

2 to talk about something that happened at an unspecified time in the past.
Fill the gaps with *already, ever* and *never*.

Have you _____ been bungee jumping? – No, _____. Have you?

I've _____ told you. Don't borrow my clothes – you don't look after them!

3 to give up-to-date news without specifying when it happened.
Note that if we give more details, we usually change tenses.

The government _____ (announce) that a number of libraries are set to close over the next year. They _____ (make) the announcement at Prime Minister's Questions yesterday.

4   to show the present result of something that happened in the unspecified past.

I can't go out with you because I _____ *(lose) my wallet. (I still don't have my wallet now.)*

Oh dear! What's happened to your leg? – I _____ *(break) it. (My leg is broken now.)*

5   with unfinished time periods.

Note that with finished time periods we use past tenses, even if a finished time period is implied but not stated, for example if we are talking about somebody no longer alive.
[The time is 10.30 am] *Poor me. I* _____ *(not have) a break this morning.*
[The time is 6.00 pm] *Poor me. I* _____ *(not have) a break this morning.*
I _____ *(be) married twice.*
Marilyn Monroe _____ *(be) married three times.*

 8
01
CD2

Answer the questions you hear so that they are true for you. Use the present perfect simple, changing tenses if appropriate.

> **Exam tip:** Be careful if your language has a tense that is constructed similarly to the present perfect tenses in English, e.g. in Latin languages. There are almost certainly some differences in the way the tenses are used. Make sure you know what the differences are.

9   **Do you know when to use the present perfect simple and when to use the present perfect continuous?**

present perfect simple	have/has + past participle e.g. **has done**
present perfect continuous	have/has + been + -ing e.g. **has been doing**

1   You can use either tense to talk about how long an activity has been going on.
I've done yoga for six years.
I've been doing yoga for six years.
The present perfect simple may be preferable if the situation is permanent or of long duration.
I've lived in Reading for twenty years.
I've been living with my mum for the past two weeks because my flat is being refurbished.

2   In other instances, only one tense is appropriate:
I've watched the film you recommended. I loved it.
The focus here is that the person has finished watching the film.
What have you been doing? – I've been watching the film you recommended.
The focus here is on the action of watching the film. We do not know if they have finished watching the film or not.

3 *I've planted some new flowers. Don't they look beautiful?*

The focus here is on the result of the planting.

Why are you covered in mud? – I've been planting some new flowers.

The focus here is on the activity that has made the person dirty. We do not know nor are we interested in whether the planting is finished or not.

4 The present perfect continuous is also used to emphasise how long something has been going on.

He tried to tell me I didn't understand the rules of the game. I've been playing badminton for twenty years. He's only been playing for three months!

Note that state verbs – e.g. *know, believe, see, want* – do not generally have a continuous form so you cannot use them in the present perfect continuous even if the meaning seems to demand it.

10 **1** **Complete the sentences with either the present perfect simple or continuous of the verbs in brackets, and where necessary *for* or *since*.**

    1 I _____ (play) the clarinet _____ I was a child.

    2 I _____ only _____ (go) scuba-diving twice.

    3 I _____ (know) her _____ three and a half years.

    4 I _____ (read) your book. You can have it back now.

    5 I _____ (watch) TV all morning. I'm so lazy!

02
CD2

2 Listen to check your answers. Then, for each question, give a reason why that tense is correct.

3 Listen to Track 02 again and repeat the sentences, focusing on your pronunciation. Pay attention to any difficult sounds, weak forms, and word and sentence stress.

03
CD2

11 Answer the questions you hear using either the present perfect simple or continuous.

IELTS Speaking Exam: Part 3

04
CD2

12 You are going to hear questions that are typical of Part 3 of the exam. Listen to each question and give your answers. Practise what you have learnt in this unit. Record your answers.

Now listen to the sample answers.

Pronunciation: The schwa /ə/

> **Exam tip:** The schwa is the most common sound in English. It cannot appear in a stressed syllable. In writing, any vowel can be used to represent it and it can be represented by more than one letter (including *r*).

🎧 13
05
CD2
Listen to the schwa sound and repeat it. Remember that to pronounce it you just relax your mouth.

🎧 14
06
CD2
1   Listen to the following words being said. For each word, underline the stressed syllable.

author	yoga
today	England
summer	Internet
collection	suppose
person	gardening
leisure	photography
famous	opinion

2   Listen to the words again. Underline in a different colour any letters that are pronounced as a schwa.

3   Check your answers, then practise saying the words. Remember not to stress the schwas.

15   Listen to the recording of your Part 3 answers. Did you use any of the words from Exercise 14? If so, did you pronounce them using the schwa? Write down ten key content words you used that you want to check the pronunciation of. Mark the stressed syllables and any schwas. Practise saying the words. Then re-record your answer, focusing on word stress and the schwa. Remember that schwas also appear in the weak forms of certain function words.

Exam technique: Sounding polite

> **Exam tip:** In all parts of the exam, you may ask the examiner to repeat the question.

07
CD2

1 Listen to these candidates. Only one sounds polite enough. Why do the other candidates sound impolite? Think about word choice and intonation.

   a Repeat, please.

   b Could you say that again, please?

   c What?

   d What did you say?

08
CD2

2 **1** Listen to the following sentence being said using both polite and impolite intonation. Can you tell which is which?

     Would you mind repeating the question?

     To sound polite, your intonation should be high and your voice should sound soft. Impolite intonation tends to be low and flat and the person's voice sounds hard.

  2 Practise saying the following sentences with a friend. Can your friend guess whether you are trying to sound polite or impolite?

     Could you say that again, please?

     Would you mind repeating the question?

09
CD2

3 In Part 3, the examiner can reformulate a question. This is useful as the questions can be complex. The following statement will signal to the examiner that you want him or her to reformulate.

   I'm sorry, I'm not sure I understand the question.

   Listen to Track 09 again and repeat the sentence, paying attention to the intonation.

10
CD2

4 You may want to indicate that you do not understand a particular word. This will show the examiner which word is preventing you from understanding the question so he or she can reformulate it effectively. Write down the sentence you hear. Check your answer, then practise saying it correctly.

5 Learn the phrases you have studied in this part so you can use them in the exam. Practise using the phrases when you next speak English.

8 Youth

Aims: Talking about remembering, childhood | Using past tenses, used to, would
Pronunciation: Past tense -ed endings, diphthongs
Exam technique: Fluency

Vocabulary: Remembering

11
CD2

1 Listen and complete the texts below with the words you hear. The words form part of collocations and phrases connected with remembering – the other words in the collocations and phrases appear in italics.

1 When I hear music from the 70s, *it really* (1) _____ *me back*. It makes me feel like I'm a teenager again, the *memories* are so (2) _____. So many things from that period of my life *left a* (3) _____ *impression on me*, like meeting my first girlfriend and sitting my A levels in sweltering heat. *It's still* (4) _____ *in my mind*.

2 *I can* (1) _____ *remember* what I did yesterday let alone events from my childhood. Well, having said that, I have some (2) _____ *memories*. I remember a teacher I really liked called ... oh, the name (3) _____ *me*. But she was so brilliant at explaining things and was really kind when my brother was taken ill. Oh, what was her name? *It's on the tip of my* (4) _____! Anyway, as I said, I have a bad memory.

3 I often reminisce about *the* (1) _____ *old days*. You have to be careful, though, because it's easy to get sentimental and see everything through rose-tinted glasses. Things weren't perfect back then but you often only remember the good times. I love looking at old photos. They remind me of people I'd (2) _____ *forgotten* about and then *it all comes* (3) _____ *back*, like my old friend Alice who passed away ten years ago. Can it really be that long? *Doesn't time* (4) _____!

2 Which phrases from Exercise 1 are paraphrased below?

1 I can almost remember it but not quite.

2 Time passes very quickly.

3 It reminds me of the past.

4 I can remember it clearly, like it was yesterday.

5 I suddenly remember it really clearly.

Vocabulary: Childhood

3 Complete sentences 1–9 with the words and collocations a–i derived from the word *child*.

a a latchkey child   d child labour   g childhood friends
b an only child   e child's play   h childish
c child benefit   f child-friendly   i happy childhood

1 I bump into my _____ occasionally though we've got nothing in common anymore.

2 I'm lucky, I had a very _____.

3 We can't take Sophie there. It's not a very _____ restaurant.

4 Does she have any brothers or sisters? – No, she's _____.

5 After your IELTS exam, that data-entry test should be _____.

6 Families with children can claim _____ from the government.

7 An estimated one in six children worldwide are engaged in _____.

8 He's _____ he arrives home from school to an empty house because his parents are at work.

9 She's older than me, yet she's so _____!

4 Match words 1–8 with definitions a–h.

1 be well brought up	**a** speak to someone angrily or seriously because they have done something wrong
2 upbringing	**b** someone who is older than you, usually someone quite a lot older
3 parenting	**c** obey a person, a command, or an instruction
4 your elders	**d** be polite because your parents have taught you to behave well
5 do as you're told	**e** do some of the housework
6 have good manners	**f** the way that your parents treat you and the things that they teach you when you are growing up
7 tell someone off	**g** the activity of bringing up and looking after your child
8 help around the house	**h** be polite and observe social customs

5 Listen to each statement. Do they reflect your experience and views? Justify your answer by giving a reason or an example.

12
CD2

Example: Most children I know are well brought up.

No, most children I know are badly brought up. They have bad manners, interrupting adults all the time and not saying please *or* thank you.

If possible, compare your experiences and views with a friend.

IELTS Speaking Exam: Part 1

6 You are going to hear questions that are typical of Part 1 of the exam. Listen to each question and give your answer. Record your answers.

13
CD2

Now listen to the sample answers.

IELTS Speaking Exam: Part 2

7 Read this Part 2 question. Give yourself one minute to plan your answer, making notes if you wish. Then talk for one or two minutes. Record your answers.

14
CD2

> **Speaking Exam Part 2**
>
> Describe a happy childhood memory.
>
> You should say:
>
> > when and where the incident you remember happened
> >
> > who you were with
> >
> > what happened exactly
>
> and explain why it is a happy memory.

Now listen to the sample answer.

Pronunciation: Past tense -*ed* endings

8 Listen to Track 15. How is -*ed* pronounced in the following regular past-tense verbs?

15
CD2

enjoy**ed**   work**ed**   act**ed**

Note that it is the final *sound* of the infinitive that decides how -*ed* is pronounced; the spelling may mislead you. Here are some rules to help guide you:

- -*ed* is pronounced /t/ when the verb ends in a voiceless consonant sound – /p/, /tʃ/, /k/, /f/, /θ/, /s/, /ʃ/.
- -*ed* is pronounced /d/ when the verb ends in a voiced consonant sound – /b/, /dʒ/, /g/, /v/, /ð/, /z/, /m/, /n/, /ŋ/, /l/ – or vowel sound. Say the sound with your fingers on your throat and you will be able to feel the vibration.
- -*ed* is pronounced /ɪd/ when the verb ends in a /d/ or a /t/ sound. This is the only time you add an extra syllable.

9 **1** Complete the table below by putting the verbs into the correct column, according to the pronunciation of -*ed*.

accepted	aged	agreed	answered	asked	breathed
cycled	decided	hated	helped	laughed	loved
matched	needed	played	pretended	seemed	thanked
wanted	wished				

/d/	/t/	/ɪd/
(handwritten answers)	*(handwritten answers)*	*(handwritten answers)*

2 Listen and check your answers. Then listen again and repeat the verbs.

10 Listen to the answers you recorded for Parts 1 and 2 in Exercises 6 and 7. Did you pronounce all the regular past-tense endings correctly? Write down any verbs you mispronounced and practise saying them correctly.

16
CD2

Pronunciation: Diphthongs

11 **1** A diphthong is a vowel sound, representing a single syllable, in which your tongue moves continuously from one position to another. Study the table below for the usual spellings and example words. Listen and repeat.

17
CD2

2 Add one more example word for each spelling. Check the pronunciation of the words you add in your dictionary because spelling can be misleading.

Vowel sounds	Usual spellings	Example words
eɪ	a (especially before consonant + *e*) ai ay	same _____ aim _____ day _____
əʊ	o (especially before consonant + *e*) oa	home _____ boat _____
aɪ	i (especially before consonant + *e*) y igh	time _____ fly _____ night _____
aʊ	ou ow	cloud _____ cow _____
ɔɪ	oi oy	choice _____ boy _____
ɪə	eer ere ear	peer _____ mere _____ hear _____
eə	air are	pair _____ stare _____

Grammar: Past tenses, *used to* and *would*

12 **1** Listen while you read the text below describing a childhood memory.

> I remember my granddad often used to take me to school when I was little. I used to live quite far from my school and my granddad let me cycle there, following behind me on foot. I kept stopping to wait for him to catch up. Then when we had arrived at school, he would push my bike home again. One day, I was cycling along happily. Suddenly I looked back and my granddad was nowhere to be seen. I waited and waited but he didn't come. I began to get worried so I cycled back the way I had come and, to my horror, found him lying on the ground. He had tripped on some loose paving. I helped him up and then took him to the doctor's, although he kept insisting he was fine. The doctor examined him and, luckily, he wasn't injured. I was so relieved and always cycled more slowly after that.

2 The text uses a variety of ways to talk about the past. Read it again and notice the different structures and tenses.

13 **1** We use *used to* + infinitive to describe past habits or past states that are now finished. The negative form is *didn't use to*.

    a Find an example in the text of *used to* to describe a past habit.
    b Find an example in the text of *used to* to describe a past state.

2 Listen again to Track 18. How is *used to* pronounced? Repeat the sentences with *used to*.

    Note that you cannot use a present form of *used to* to talk about present habits, e.g. ~~I use to travel to university by car~~. Just use the present simple: *I travel to university by car*.

3 We can also use *would* + infinitive to describe past habits. However, we cannot use it to describe extended past states. The negative form is rarely used.

    a Find an example in the text of *would* to describe a past habit.
    b Listen to Track 18 again and notice how *would* is pronounced.

14 We can also use the past simple to describe past habits or past states. The past simple has other uses: to describe single completed actions in the past, or a series of actions in the order they took place.

    1 Read the text in Exercise 12 again and find the first example of:

      a the past simple used to describe a past state _____
      b the past simple used to describe a past habit _____
      c the past simple used to describe a single completed action. _____

    2 There is one mistake in each set of sentences below. Find what is wrong, say why, and correct the mistakes.

      a When I was a little girl, I would see my cousin every weekend and going with him to the local park.

      b Years ago I would own a horse. I loved riding her but she was expensive to keep so I had to sell her.

      c Last week I used to see Sam at the cinema. He didn't say 'hello' to me, probably because he felt awkward as he was with his new girlfriend.

Exam tip: Use *used to*, *would* and the past simple to talk about things that you did when you were younger that you no longer do, or to describe situations that are no longer true. Below are some ideas for topics. Record yourself and pay attention to your pronunciation.

where you lived	pets you had	your pastimes
toys you played with	friends you had	your daily routine

15 The past continuous (*was/were* + *-ing*) tells us that something was in progress at a particular time in the past. We can use the past simple for an action that interrupted or happened during the past continuous action. The past continuous is also used to give the background to a story.

    1 Find an example in the text in Exercise 12 of the past continuous being used to give background. Which main action does it give the background to?

    2 Listen to Track 18 again. Notice that the speaker uses the weak form of *was*. Practise saying these sentences using the weak forms.

        I **was** /wəz/ *cycling along.*   *They* **were** /wə/ *cycling along.*

Note that the past continuous is not generally used with state verbs, e.g. ~~I was liking the meal~~. It does not normally describe repeated actions or habits in the past, e.g. ~~When I was a child, we were having dinner together as a family.~~

    3 Complete the sentences with the past continuous or the past simple of the verbs in brackets.

        a One day, my cousin and I (1) _____ (*jump*) up and down on my bed. We (2) _____ (*enjoy*) ourselves immensely but then my mum (3) _____ (*walk*) in and (4) _____ (*tell*) us off.

        b I (1) _____ (*be*) on holiday with my family and we (2) _____ (*walk*) along the beach. Suddenly a dog (3) _____ (*run*) up to us. It (4) _____ (*bark*) aggressively and we (5) _____ (*be*) terrified. My dad (6) _____ (*try*) to scare it off but it (7) _____ (*bite*) him.

16 We use the past perfect simple (*had* + past participle) to say something happened before something else in the past – it is 'more past'. Notice the difference between the following two sentences:

When I arrived, my friend **opened** *her presents.* (= *I arrived, then my friend opened her presents. The actions are described chronologically.*)

When I arrived, my friend **had opened** *her presents.* OR *My friend* **had opened** *her presents when I arrived.* (= *My friend opened her presents before I arrived.*)

    1 Find an example in the text in Exercise 12 of the past simple used to describe a single action in the past and the past perfect used to describe something 'more past' than that action.

    2 There are two possible weak forms of *had*: /həd/ and /əd/. You can also use the contraction *'d*. Practise saying these sentences:

        He **had** /həd/ *tripped.*   *He* **had** /əd/ *tripped.*   **He'd** /hiːd/ *tripped.*

3 Complete the sentences with the past continuous, the past simple or the past perfect of the verbs in brackets.

One day my sister, Madoka, (1) _____ (play) out in the garden, throwing a tennis ball against the wall of the house. She (2) _____ (be) a bit careless and suddenly I (3) _____ (hear) a smash. I (4) _____ (go) outside and (5) _____ (see) that she (6) _____ (break) the window. Just at that moment, our mum (7) _____ (arrive) home from work. She (8) _____ (say) 'hello' to us cheerfully and then (9) _____ (look) over at the window and (10) _____ (gasp) in horror. She (11) _____ (realise) straight away what (12) _____ (happen), but she (13) _____ (blame) me because she (14) _____ (ask) me not to leave my sister alone. I (15) _____ (be) so angry with Madoka!

17 **1** Listen to your Part 2 recording for Track 14 (page 66). How accurate were you in your use of tenses (past simple, past continuous and past perfect) and structures (*would, used to*)? Did you use a range of language or, for example, did you just use the past simple?

2 Re-record your answer, trying to improve your accuracy and range.

Exam tip: To do well in the exam it is vital for you to be a self-aware learner. Recording your answers will allow you to increase your self-awareness. You cannot concentrate on every element of your English while you are speaking, but by listening to yourself afterwards you can:

- identify your strong points and your weak points in grammar, vocabulary, pronunciation, fluency and coherence
- ask a friend or teacher to listen and comment on your performance
- hear where you have gaps in your knowledge of grammar or vocabulary
- improve your knowledge and then re-record your answer
- see how you have improved by comparing your performance with earlier recordings, which will boost your confidence.

IELTS Speaking Exam: Part 3

18 You are going to hear questions that are typical of Part 3 of the exam. Listen to each question and give your answers. Record your answers.

Listen to your recording, assessing your use of the vocabulary, grammar and pronunciation you have studied in this unit. Re-record your answers, trying to improve your performance in the areas where you were weaker.

Now listen to the sample answers.

19
CD2

Exam technique: Fluency

Exam tip: Fluency, together with coherence, makes up a quarter of your mark. The examiners will judge you to be 'fluent' if you:
- speak continuously – that is, you do not leave big pauses or hesitate too often
- speak at a good rate – that is, not too slowly.

Improving fluency takes time. The most important thing is to **speak as much as possible**. Doing all the speaking activities in this book will certainly make you more fluent. Here are some other ideas:

- Having good pronunciation improves your fluency because it allows you to speak more quickly without making you unclear. The pronunciation of single sounds and single words, word and sentence stress, and connected speech are all crucial. Study the pronunciation points in this book carefully.

- Having a wide-ranging vocabulary allows you to be more fluent because you do not have to hesitate, trying to find the right word. Having good grammar has a similar effect. If your grammar and vocabulary are good, you can focus more on your ideas.

- Find out if there is an English conversation class in your local area. If one exists, join it. Speaking English regularly, and in front of other people, will improve your confidence as well as your grammar, vocabulary, pronunciation and, of course, your fluency.

- Meet up with an English-speaking friend and study this book with them. In addition, agree that for one hour every week you will speak only in English. Be strict with yourselves: do not speak even one word of your mother tongue or any other language, and do not consult your dictionaries. This will force you to express yourself in English even if it is sometimes difficult.

- As you do daily tasks, talk to yourself in English (aloud or in your head). Think, *How do you say that in English?* This will give you extra practice in thinking in English, and will make speaking it less of an effort. The examiner will also judge how much *effort* it takes you to speak in English. If you seem to be unpractised at using English to express yourself, you will not score well for fluency.

Fluency is largely a matter of **confidence**. A confident speaker is more fluent because they are less self-conscious. Practising speaking English will make you more confident. In addition, think about your **body language** and ensure you *look* confident:

- Smile when you first meet the examiner and when you introduce yourself.

- Look the examiner in the eye as you speak. Do not look down.

- Do not sit with your arms crossed as this will make you look defensive and nervous.

- Do not fidget.

- Ask a friend to interview you. Do they think you appear confident and relaxed? Why or why not?

9 Home

Vocabulary: Describing places

1 **1** Would you rather live in a city or in the country?

  2 Decide if sentences 1–6 refer to the city or the country.

  1 Urban regeneration involves bringing derelict buildings back into use.

  2 It's very remote.

  3 I live right in the centre, within easy walking distance of shops, restaurants and bars.

  4 I like living here because I love all the hustle and bustle.

  5 Where my auntie lives is idyllic and the pace of life is very slow.

  6 You don't see many detached houses here. It's all high-rise flats.

2 Complete the sentences below with words a–n.

a backwater	b far	c middle	d easy	e picturesque

My village is:
  in the (1) _____ C _____ of nowhere.
  a real (2) _____ a _____.
  within (3) _____ d _____ reach of the nearest big town/city.
  not (4) _____ b _____ from a big town/city.
  idyllic and the countryside is really (5) _____ e _____.

f congested	g cosmopolitan	h destination

My city/town is:
  very (6) _____ g _____. You can meet people from all over the world.
  a tourist (7) _____ h _____.
  pretty polluted and (8) _____ f _____.

| i | spacious | k | heart | m | outskirts |
| j | walking | l | cramped | n | suburbs |

My house is:
(9) _____. I wish it was bigger.
big and (10) _____.
in the (11) _____
on the (12) _____ of a town called Sopron.
right in the (13) _____ of the village.
within (14) _____ distance of the local shop.

3 Use any appropriate vocabulary above to practise talking about where you live. After each sentence add extra details that explain what you have said.

Example: My city is very cosmopolitan. We have people from all over the world living here, and that's reflected in the cuisine. You can eat lots of different types of food.

In addition, you can use this vocabulary to talk about your home.

I live in a:
detached/semi-detached/terraced house.
bungalow.
maisonette.
ground-/first-/second-/top-floor flat.
Practise once, then practise again without looking at the vocabulary.

Vocabulary: Comparing now and then

4 **20 CD2**

1 **Listen and complete the texts about changes to the speakers' hometowns.**

1 (1) _____, this was a nice place to live. Everyone knew everyone and people looked out for each other. I'm sorry to say that, (2) _____, the population has risen dramatically and this has led to a breakdown in the community ties that used to unite us. Also, second-home owners buy holiday homes here, and that has meant that the price of property has escalated (3) _____, forcing young people to move away from the area.

2 My city is becoming more and more vibrant (1) _____. I love it! (2) _____ really dull, with nothing much for young people to do, (3) _____ bars and clubs have begun opening up. The city's no longer just for the older generations, with theatres and museums – it's got a new lease of life, with a great nightlife and an increasing student population to enjoy it.

3 (1) _____, this town was a hive of activity, with its many factories and its port. (2) _____, however, it's nowhere near as bustling, as manufacturing has moved elsewhere. But I for one don't bewail the changes. There's a certain poignancy and beauty to the disused industrial architecture. And, in fact, many of the old factories (3) _____ into flats, and they're extremely popular with trendy young couples who are now moving into the town.

2 Listen to Track 20 again.
  a What tense is used to describe how things were in the past?
  b What tenses are used to describe the current situation?

5

IELTS Speaking Exam: Part 1

You are going to hear questions that are typical of Part 1 of the exam. Listen to each question and give your answers. Try to use the vocabulary you have learnt so far. Focus on your use of tenses, particularly when talking about changes to your town or city.

Now listen to the sample answers.

> **Exam tip:** It is perfectly acceptable to say negative things about your hometown or any other topic – for example, *There is not much for young people to do* or *It used to be peaceful but now it's built up and congested.* However, focusing exclusively or almost exclusively on the negative in all your answers will affect the impression the examiner gains of you. Although you will not be judged specifically on your attitudes, it is probably better to present yourself as a predominantly positive person.

Vocabulary: Suffixes

> **Exam tip:** Suffixes are letters added to the end of a word to form another word, e.g. *possibility*. *Possible* is an adjective and adding *-ity* turns it into a noun. Using suffixes allows you to make new words from words you already know, dramatically improving your ability to express yourself.

6

1 Add the following suffixes to words 1–12 below to make nouns. Use each suffix twice.

-ness -ee -ism -hood -ment -ship

1 mother_____	**5** alcohol_____	**9** disappoint_____
2 forgetful_____	**6** craftsman_____	**10** hero_____
3 address_____	**7** aware_____	**11** leader_____
4 treat_____	**8** employ_____	**12** neighbour_____

2 Write down at least two more words formed using each suffix.

Example: –ment: management, understatement

Other noun suffixes include *-ence/-ance* (independence), *-tion/-sion* (information), *-age* (marriage), *-y* (efficiency), *-(e)ry* (misery), and *-ant* (assistant).

3 Complete sentences 1–5 with the noun form of the words in brackets.

  1 There is a real _____ of affordable housing in my town. (short)
  2 Fortunately there is almost full _____ in this part of the country. (employ)
  3 The _____ of natural resources means we have to import an awful amount. (scarce)
  4 _____ is quite common when you're away from home for long periods. (homesick)
  5 I have a _____ for flats over bungalows. (prefer)

7 **1** Forming adjectives: Put the noun roots below in the correct gaps to form adjectives. Take care with any spelling changes.

road   mess   mountain   plenty   child

1 This region is extremely _____ous.
2 My car is not _____worthy at the moment, so I'll have to take the bus home.
3 Our home is completely _____proof. We've had to make sure of that since having Jake.
4 Our house is always _____y because none of us is very house-proud.
5 We have a _____ful supply of organic produce due to the large number of farms in the surrounding area.

2 Write down at least two more examples of adjectives formed with the suffixes above.

Other suffixes used to form adjectives include -ible/-able (breakable), -ive (attractive), -ish (smallish), and -al (optional).

8 **1** Using the suffixes -ise, -en, or –ify below, complete sentences 1–5 with the verb form of the word in brackets. Ensure the verbs are in the correct tense.

1 Sadly, my mum was _____ last week. It means I'm having to do all the housework. (hospital)
2 I would _____ my uncle's house as 'a mansion'. (class)
3 Driving to the shops _____ the journey by twenty minutes but I prefer to walk because it's healthier. (short)
4 They've _____ the motorway because it was always so congested. (wide)
5 The local council is trying to _____ the city by planting flowers and cleaning up. (beauty)

2 Find at least two more examples of verbs formed using each of the suffixes. Another typical verb suffix is -ate, as in abbreviate. How many more verbs ending in -ate do you know?

IELTS Speaking Exam: Part 2

🎧 **9** Read this Part 2 question. Give yourself one minute to plan your answer, making notes if
22   you wish. Then talk for one or two minutes. Practise using the vocabulary you have learnt
CD2   so far in this unit.

Describe a place that you enjoy visiting.

You should say:

    where the place is

    what you can see and do there

      how it has changed since you first visited it

and explain why you enjoy visiting this place.

Now listen to the sample answers.

Pronunciation: Silent letters

10 **1** Do you know how to pronounce these English towns and cities? It may not be as you expect because they are not pronounced exactly as they are written. Only one of these place names is pronounced as you would probably expect. What is it?

Leicester   Newcastle   Reading   Greenwich   Plymouth   Cambridge

23
CD2

2 Listen and underline the letters representing the following sounds:

a /e/ (there are three)
b the schwa, /ə/ (there are two)
c the diphthong /eɪ/ (there is one).

3 Listen to Track 23 again. Notice that in the first four place names some letters are not pronounced.

11 **1** There are a large number of words in English with silent letters. For this reason it is important to learn the pronunciation of words, not just guess the pronunciation from the way the words are spelt. Highlight the silent letters in words 1–10 below.

1	island	6	vineyard
2	calm	7	walk
3	camera	8	Wednesday
4	half	9	foreigner
5	interesting	10	restaurant

24
CD2

2 Listen to check your answers. Then repeat the words.

25
CD2

IELTS Speaking Exam: Part 3

12 You are going to hear questions that are typical of Part 3 of the exam. Answer them and record your answers. Ask a friend or teacher to listen carefully to your recording. Are there any words you pronounced incorrectly? Practise saying the words with accurate pronunciation. Keep a list of words you have mispronounced and test yourself frequently.

Now listen to the sample answers.

Exam tip: You will have noticed that the sample answers contain contractions, e.g. *I'm* (for *I am*). Contractions are extremely common in spoken English, and using them can make your English sound more natural and fluent. Check how to pronounce them, however, or your English could become unclear.

Some contractions are very informal and are better avoided in the exam, e.g. *ain't* and *init* (for *isn't it*). Studying the sample answers will show you which contractions are suitable.

Grammar: The passive

13 You can use the passive (*be* + past participle) to introduce an argument or opinion. The impersonal subject *it* is often used. Study these examples.

> *It is* often **argued that** *communities are breaking down.* (*it + be* + past participle + *that ...*)

> *Saint Petersburg is considered* by many **to be** *Russia's most beautiful city.* (subject + *be* + past participle + *to* infinitive)

We use the passive if the performer of the action is unimportant or unknown.

Other verbs typical in this type of construction are *believe, say, think, find, claim, reported, prove,* and *show.* Example: *It has been conclusively shown that children benefit from a stable home environment.*

Decide if the following sentences can be rewritten in the passive. If so, rewrite them. (Note that none of the sentences below is incorrect and that the use of the passive is optional.)

a People say that my local Italian is the best restaurant in town.
b My mum thinks a country lifestyle is best.
c They have found that the new canal is a flood risk.

14 Similar passive constructions can be used to introduce others' views. Then you can say why you do not agree.

> **Although** *the city's National Gallery* **is** *often* **thought to be** *the most interesting gallery,* **I prefer** *the Modern Art Gallery.*

> **It could be argued that** *cities are dangerous places,* **but I think** *that if you're streetwise that needn't be the case.*

Complete the sentences below so they are true for you.

a Although _____ is usually considered to be the most beautiful region in my country, I _____.
b Home cooking/Restaurant food is often thought to be superior to restaurant food/home cooking, but, in my opinion, _____.
c It could be argued that it is better to live in the city/country than in the country/city, but I _____.

15 You can also form the passive with *get* + past participle. This is more informal than the passive with *be*. We can use *get* to express misfortune or something unexpected:

> *I* **got made** *redundant last month.*
> or to express an achievement:
> *I* **got accepted** *into university.*

In which sentences below are we likely to use a form of *get*?

a I was talking to the gas company but I **was** cut off.
b My dad **was** elected as leader of the local council.
c The town centre **is being** regenerated.

Grammar: The causative

16 We use *have something done* to describe something that is done to us rather than us doing it ourselves. It often describes a service that we have arranged someone else to do for us:

> *I'm **having** my hair **cut** next week.* My hairdresser is cutting my hair next week:

but it may also describe something unpleasant and out of your control:

> *I've **had** my pay **frozen**.* My boss has frozen my pay:

It is usually unnecessary to say who performs the service, but if we want to give this information, we add *by* + agent, e.g. *by my boss*.

Instead of *have*, we can use *get*. It is slightly more informal.

1 Re-write these sentences using the causative.

  a A decorator is repainting our lounge.

  We _____.

  b A sculptor made a statue of Shakespeare for the council.

  The council ...

  c A burglar burgled my house.

  I _____.

  d Our house is far too small, so a builder is going to build an extension.

  Our house is far too small, so we _____.

2 Now practise talking about something you have had done recently, or are having done soon.

Exam technique: Clarifying, paraphrasing and giving examples

> **Exam tip:** You will be judged on how successfully you are able to paraphrase in the exam. You may want to, or be asked to, repeat what you have said but in a different way, or you may want to clarify what you have said.
>
> To paraphrase well, you need to have a wide range of synonyms at your command, but knowing some phrases to introduce your rephrasing will also help.

If you think you have not expressed something exactly right, you can reformulate using the phrase in bold below.

> *Patriotism is a terrible thing.* **Let me rephrase that**: *patriotism is not always a force for good.*

You could also say, **Or, more accurately, ...**

1

1   Listen to both phrases being used, and repeat.

2   Why do you think this candidate wanted to rephrase the first sentence?

To explain more fully a point you have made, you can use the following phrase:

> *My house is too small.* **What I mean is that** *it is too small for our family, because there are so many of us. For an average-sized family it would do very well.*

You could also say **Or, to put it another way, ...**

2

1   Listen to both phrases being used, and repeat.

2   Is this speaker's house big or small?

To say something in a different way, especially a clearer or simpler way, use the phrase below.

> *People from my village are suspicious of foreigners.* **In other words,** *they're xenophobic.*

3   Listen and repeat.

You will often want to illustrate your argument with an example. You will be familiar with the phrases *for example* and *for instance*, but note that they do not have to come at the beginning of a sentence.

4   **Where do you think the speakers insert the phrases? Listen to check.**

> *People in the past were not so mobile. My grandparents lived all their lives in the town where they were born.*
>
> *People in my country like foreign cuisine. Korean restaurants are very popular as are Chinese restaurants.*

5   Learn the phrases in this section and use them when answering the practice exam questions.

10 Culture

Vocabulary: Festivals and historical sites

1   Match questions 1–4 to answers a–d.

1 How is it celebrated?	a On November 8th the whole country has a huge celebration.
2 What is it in honour of?	b It marks the anniversary of the day that we gained our independence.
3 Do you enjoy it?	c We all get the day off, and we march through the streets holding banners and singing our national anthem. Then we hold street parties, eating traditional food and having fun. At night, fireworks are set off. The parties go on till the small hours of the morning.
4 What is your country's biggest festival?	d Very much so. The build-up to it is so exciting, and on the day itself everyone's always in a great mood.

2   Complete the text below with words a–g from Exercise 1.

  a day off   **d** national anthem   **f** marks
  b celebrations   **e** banners   **g** anniversary
  c street parties

The 20th of May (1) _____ the (2) _____ of when our King
ascended to the throne. Every year there are massive (3) _____ in every city,
town and village throughout the country. All workers are granted the
(4) _____ and the rules around having (5) _____ are relaxed
making it easier for people to close off the roads to traffic, set up stalls and put up
(6) _____. In the afternoon, we all watch a television address by the King, and
then our (7) _____ is performed. Everyone knows the words, of course, so we
all sing along.

3   Choose the correct words in italics 1–12 to complete the text.

It's all too unusual for archeology to make the news but the other day there was a news
item about an (1) *excavation/exhumation* not far from where I live. An archeologist proudly
announced that he and his team had found the (2) *leftovers/remains* of a group of Bronze
Age roundhouses. In fact, all they had (3) *displayed/unearthed* of the buildings themselves
were post-holes, but they were clearly chuffed by the discovery. They had also found a
large number of (4) *ruins/artefacts*, and by carbon dating some substance from inside a
pot they were able to (5) *date/time* the site to around 2000 (6) *BC/AD*. Although people tend
to think of prehistoric man as (7) *illiterate/primitive*, the archeologist explained that they
were more sophisticated than we many imagine, capable of creating the most elaborate
metalwork, both (8) *ornaments/embroidery* and weapons. And Neolithic man was
clever enough to (9) *demolish/construct* structures such as Stonehenge, which still
(10) *draws/pulls* over 800,000 visitors each year. The (11) *finds/findings* will be
(12) *exposed/exhibited* in my local museum and I'll definitely go to see them.

Vocabulary: Protecting our heritage

4   1   Read the following text.

> In the UK, our **heritage** is protected with the help of the system of listing buildings. A
> **listed building** is one that is considered to have **historical significance**. It cannot be
> **altered** or **demolished** without **permission** from the **local planning authority**. As well
> as houses, other structures can also be **protected**, such as bridges and even bunkers.

  2   Do you have a similar system in your country? Research the topic and practise talking
      about it, using some of the vocabulary in bold above.

5   1   Read the text below.

> UNESCO helps protect the world's **natural and cultural heritage** by designating
> places as UNESCO **World Heritage Sites**. Such a **designation** means that the site is
> considered of great importance to the common heritage of mankind. The sites can
> sometimes receive **funding**. Examples of World Heritage Sites are the Pyramids of
> Giza, Venice and the Statue of Liberty.

2 What is your nearest World Heritage Site? Have you visited it? Do some research on the topic and practise talking about it, using some of the vocabulary in bold above.

IELTS Speaking Exam: Part 1

6 You are going to hear some questions that are typical of Part 1 of the exam. Listen to the questions and record yourself answering them.

Now listen to the sample answers.

Pronunciation: Linking

7 **1** Record yourself reading the sample answer to the first Part 1 question, beginning *Our most important festival is without doubt* ...

2 Now listen to the sample answer on Track 31. Does the speech sound natural?

Listen to a second reading of the same sample answer on Track 32. How does it compare with the first?

3 Play your recording. Is it more similar to Track 31 or Track 32?

The speaker in Track 32 sounds more fluent partly because her linking is effective. Below we look at some of the rules governing linking in normal speech.

8 **1** Consonant + vowel

Listen:

in␣␣␣␣England   most␣␣␣␣important

Where one word ends in a consonant sound and the next word begins with a vowel sound, we do not pause between the words – we link the words.

2 Vowel + vowel

a Listen. What sound is inserted between the two vowel sounds?
- the   end
- I   ate

We add an extra sound, / ____ /, to link two vowel sounds when the first vowel is /eɪ/, /aɪ/, /ɔɪ/ or /iː/.

b Listen. What sound is inserted between the two vowel sounds? Complete the sentence below.
- too   often
- so   amazing

We add an extra sound, / ___ /, to link two vowel sounds when the first vowel is /aʊ/, /əʊ/ or /uː/.

36
CD2

c   Listen. Which sound links the words below? Complete the sentences below.

- fa**r a**way
- I sa**w i**t

We add an extra sound, / _____ /, to link a word ending in *r* or *re* and a word beginning with a vowel. (Note that in many English accents, including standard British English, final *r* or *re* is not pronounced so these words end in a vowel sound.)

Many speakers also add / _____ / to link two vowel sounds when the first vowel is /ɪə/, /eə/, /ʊə/, /ɔː/, /ɜː/, /ɑː/ or /ə/.

3   Practise linking all the words above correctly.

9

1   Read Tracks 31 and 32 on page 123 and mark the words that should be linked.

2   Check your answers in the Answer key. Then practise reading the text, linking the words appropriately. Remember to pronounce any weak forms correctly, as well, e.g. *for, and, were*. Record yourself.

3   Listen to your initial recording of the sample answer. Have you improved?

4   Listen to your own Part 1 answers. Then answer the questions again, making an attempt to link words where appropriate.

IELTS Speaking Exam: Part 2

37
CD2

10   Read this Part 2 question. Give yourself one minute to plan your answer, making notes if you wish. Then talk for one to two minutes. Try to use some of the vocabulary you have learnt on the topic of festivals.

> Describe a festival that you enjoy.
>
> You should say:
>
>   when the festival occurs
>
>   where it occurs
>
>   what happens during it
>
> and explain why you enjoy the festival.

Now listen to the sample answer.

Grammar and pronunciation: The future

11 **1** Listen to this person talking about New Year and her plans.

38
CD2

2 Listen again and write down what she says. What tense does she use? Underline once where the tense is used to describe the future, and twice where it is used to describe the present.

3 When referring to the future, the present continuous describes a fixed arrangement, something that has been organised with another person, or a company or organisation. Study these examples:

> We're **flying** to France next week. (We have arranged it with the airline – we have bought our tickets.)
>
> I'm **meeting** my friend John for lunch today. (I have arranged it with John – we have decided on a place and time.)
>
> My mum's **starting** her new job on Monday. (She's arranged it with her new boss – she's been offered the job and told when to start.)

What preparations may the speaker in Track 38 have made for her trip?

12 **1** Listen to the example sentences above being spoken.

39
CD2

2 Listen to the contractions and practise pronouncing them.

40
CD2

Contraction	Pronunciation
I'm	/aɪm/
it's	/s/ after /f/, /k/, /p/, /t/, /θ/
he's/she's	/z/ after other sounds
you're	/jɔː/ or (weak form) /jə/
they're	/ðeə/
we're	/wɪə/

13 **1** You can also use *be going + to* infinitive to talk about future plans. In many cases, both the present continuous and *be going to* can be used. However, there are times when one tense is more appropriate. *Be going to* emphasises a previous decision or intention. Study these examples:

> I'm **going to take** a long lunch break today.
> I think my boss **is going to sack** me – he's called me in to see him urgently.
> We're **going to move** house next year.
> Note that *be going to go* is usually abbreviated to *be going*, e.g. We're going ~~to go~~ to Japan.

2 *Be going to* has another use – that of predicting something based on current evidence:

    a *England **are going to lose** in the cricket again.*

    b *That woman'**s going to trip**.*

    c *Do you think it'**s going to snow**? – Yes, definitely.*

What could be the possible evidence for the predictions above?

41
CD2

3 Listen to the three sentences above being spoken. In which sentence is *going to* pronounced /gənə/? Native speakers very often use this weak form. It is more informal than the full form.

14 **1** *Will* + infinitive (or *won't* + infinitive) is used with predictions based on opinions or our experience, with hopes and with assumptions. Study these examples:

    1 *He'**ll call** you when he gets there. Don't worry.*

    2 *I hope we'**ll be able** to go out today – it hasn't stopped raining.*

    3 *In the future, people **will live** for much longer than they do now.*
    and with future events that are not yet arranged:

    4 *I think I'**ll visit** my grandmother this weekend.*
    We also use *will* for spontaneous offers or decisions.

    5 *I'm not sure I follow you. – I'**ll explain** it again.*

42
CD2

2 Listen to the sentences above, paying particular attention to the pronunciation of the contraction *'ll*. Repeat what you hear.

15 **1** **Choose the correct future forms in bold to complete the dialogue.**

    Sarah: (1) **Are you doing/Will you do** anything special for New Year?

    Laura: Well, I might go to Granada. (2) **I'm looking/I'm going to look** online tonight to try and find a good last-minute deal. I kept tonight free on purpose because I know these things take ages!

    Sarah: Oh, don't worry. (3) **I'm going to help/I'll help** you.

    Laura: Oh, brilliant. Thanks. How about you? (4) **Are you going/Will you go** away?

    Sarah: Yes. Steve and I (5) **are spending/will spend** two weeks with my parents in Scotland.

    Laura: Oh, that (6) **is going to be/will be** lovely.

2 **Practise talking about the future with a friend. Below are some ideas for topics:**

- your plans for the weekend and for New Year/Christmas/your birthday
- the future plans of people you know
- the weather tomorrow/next week
- some current news/sports stories (predict how they will develop)

Example: You know that volcanic eruption? I don't think they'll find any survivors. Do you?

16 The future perfect – *will have* + past participle – is used to say something will have happened or will have been completed by a certain point in the future (note that *by* here means *not later than*). The weak forms of *will have* are /wɪl həv/ or /wɪl əv/.

1 Listen and complete the sentence with the words you hear.

People in my country are becoming less religious, so I think that by 2050 people _____ about the origins of Christmas.

2 Use the following phrases to make some predictions about things that will have happened or been completed by a certain point in the future.

- By this time next year . . .
- By the time I retire . . .
- By the year 2050 . . .
- By the next millennium . . .

> **Exam tip:** The IELTS exam is designed to challenge even the best students, so don't worry if you struggle at some point in the exam. This is completely normal and the examiner will expect it.
>
> It is better to be honest if you don't understand a question. And if you need some time to think before you answer a question, don't sit in silence with no explanation. Say something like, *Let me just think about that for a moment.*

IELTS Speaking Exam: Part 3

17 You are going to hear questions that are typical of Part 3 of the exam. Listen and answer the questions, practising what you have learnt in this unit, paying particular attention to your use of future forms.

Now listen to the sample answer.

Exam technique: Predicting questions

Exam tip: There is almost an infinite number of possible questions for Part 3 of the exam. It is therefore useful for you to be able to predict questions based on topical issues you may encounter, for example in the news. The following exercises will guide you in generating possible questions and allow you to train on any topic. These techniques can also help you during the exam to anticipate the examiner's next question.

1 Look at this brainstorm on the topic of celebrity.

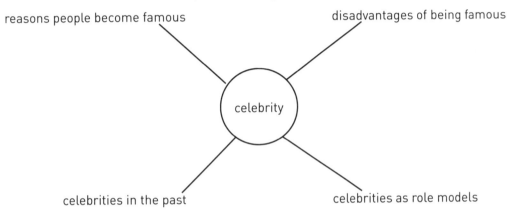

reasons people become famous

disadvantages of being famous

celebrity

celebrities in the past

celebrities as role models

With a friend if possible, brainstorm the following topics:
- the media
- advertising
- food

2 Look carefully at all the Part 3 questions you have studied so far in this book. Notice that Part 3 questions often ask you to:
- compare the present with the past
- predict how things will change in the future
- speculate about and analyse issues

and you are often asked to talk about issues within the context of your own country.

With the above points in mind, write three possible Part 3 questions on each of the topics brainstormed above. Then practise answering them, with a friend acting as the examiner.

Celebrity   Advertising
The media   Food

11 On the move

Vocabulary: Holidays

1   1   Match questions 1–5 to their responses a–e.

1 Did you get **a package deal**? _____	**a** No, I'm too old for that now. I don't want to **rough** it anymore!
2 Oh, you're going round Europe. Are you going **backpacking** again? _____	**b** Well, **eating out** is so expensive.
3 Have you **booked** your holiday already? _____	**c** Yes, we go often because we've got **a holiday home** there.
4 Are you going to Italy again? _____	**d**. No, we booked our flights and accommodation separately. It was actually cheaper that way.
5 How come you decided to **go self-catering**? _____	**e** No, we're going to try and get **a last-minute deal**.

2   Look up the meanings of the words and phrases in bold and make a note of them.

2 **1** Tick the activities you have done on holiday.

going sightseeing ☐	sunbathing ☐	going on excursions	☐
relaxing ☐	eating out ☐	visiting museums and galleries	☐
shopping ☐	going hiking ☐	sampling the local nightlife	☐

2 For each activity you have enjoyed, say when and where you did it and what you liked about it.

Example: I went sightseeing last year when I was in Beijing. It was awe-inspiring because everything was on such a grand scale, though admittedly it was also tiring because we covered a lot of ground.

3 For each activity you have not done or do not like, say why.

Example: I don't really enjoy sunbathing because I get burnt really easily. I tend to sit in the shade and read instead.

4 Talk to an English-speaking friend about what you like, and don't like, to do on holiday, and why. How do your tastes differ? Would you enjoy going on holiday together?

Vocabulary: Tourism

3 **1** Consider the impact each of the following has on tourism, especially in developing countries. In each case, decide whether it is the economy, environment, or local people that are most affected and say whether the impact is positive or negative.

   a Hotels are built on previously unspoilt beaches.
   b Tourism can bring higher levels of employment.
   c There is increased investment, especially from foreign companies.
   d There is improved infrastructure, such as roads and airports.
   e Jobs in tourism are often low paid and seasonal.
   f Tourists drop litter and cause footpath erosion.
   g Big hotels and tourist sites may take trade away from smaller businesses.
   h Income from tourism can go into conserving the natural environment.

2 Which words in Exercise 3.1 are defined below?

   a happening only for a certain part of the year
   b the wearing away of soil or rocks
   c beautiful because it has not been changed/damaged by people
   d business activity

3 What effects has tourism had on your country? What effects has tourism had on countries you have visited? Do some research and discuss with a friend.

Grammar: Short answers

4 **1** When the examiner asks you a yes/no question, you can begin your response with a short answer. Saying just *yes* or *no* sounds abrupt. In addition, using short answers correctly is one way of showing the examiner you have a good grasp of English.

Yes answers consist of: *Yes* + subject + auxiliary verb or *be*.

- *Do you enjoy going on holiday with your parents? Yes, I* **do**.
- *Can you afford to go on holiday this year? Yes, we* **can**.
- *Were you skiing when you fell? Yes, I* **was**.
- *Are you sure? Yes, I* **am**.

2 Do not use contracted forms in *yes* answers: Yes, I'm./Yes, they've./Yes, we're.

3 You can use other words in short answers:

- *Yes, I* **certainly** *do*.
- *Yes, we can –* **just about**.
- **Of course** *I am*.
- *I'm* **pretty sure** *she is*.

4 Or you can use other phrases:

- *Did your mum enjoy her holiday? I believe so, yes.*
- *Would you go back again? Definitely.*
- *Would you recommend it? Without a doubt.*

5 You can use *do, does, did* to respond to statements or questions with no auxiliary verb or non-auxiliary *be*:

- *So, your sister likes action-packed holidays. Yes, she* **does**.
- *Many people prefer relaxing holidays. I suppose they* **do**.

6 For *no* answers, we usually use the contracted form:

- *So, you* **didn't** *enjoy that holiday. I* **didn't**, *no*.
- *Has she got travel insurance? No, she* **hasn't**.
- *Are they from your hometown? No, they* **aren't**.
- *Are you going on holiday soon? I'm* **not**, *unfortunately*.

7 You can use other phrases to respond negatively:

- *Is it hot in Norway in the spring? I don't* **think so**.
- *Do you enjoy camping? No,* **not really**.
- *Do the local people benefit from tourism? I* **doubt it**.
- *Would you ever go on a skiing holiday?* **Definitely not!**

 5 **Listen to the questions and statements. Respond using a short answer and give some more details.**

45
CD2

Example: Have you been on holiday yet this year? – No, I haven't, but I plan to go and see my family in Iran later in the year. I'm really looking forward to it because I know they'll spoil me rotten!

IELTS Speaking Exam: Part 1

6   You are going to hear questions that are typical of Part 1 of the exam. Listen to each question and give your answer. Use short answers where appropriate.

Now listen to the sample answers.

Expressing yourself indirectly

> **Exam tip:** If you don't know the word for something, you will need to express it in an indirect way. For example, if you don't know the term *brochure*, instead of *We looked in a travel brochure*, you could say *We looked in a magazine with information about all kinds of holidays.*

7   **1**   Match the beginnings of sentences 1–8 with the endings a–h.

1 It's a kind of … _____	**a** sells you flights and accommodation.
2 It's something you do when … _____	**b** keeping your toothbrush, shower gel and brush in.
3 It's made of … _____	**c** short holiday.
4 It's a place where … _____	**d** a pair of shorts but it's for swimming in.
5 It's something you … _____	**e** cardboard, with a picture and room to write on the other side.
6 It looks (a bit) like … _____	**f** wear on your feet on the beach.
7 It's used for … _____	**g** you want to get a tan.
8 It's a person who … _____	**h** young people can stay cheaply.

2   What do you think is being described each time? Check your answers, then cover the phrases above and, if possible, practise describing the things to a friend. Can they guess what you are describing?

You can also use these phrases to explain words or concepts from your own language for which there is no direct translation.

8   Describe the words below indirectly using the phrases 1–8 from Exercise 7. Ask someone to guess what you are describing. Practise with more words if you like.

a passenger   camping   a suitcase   a port   an excursion

47
CD2

IELTS Speaking Exam: Part 2

9 Read this Part 2 question. Give yourself one minute to plan your answer, making notes if you wish. Then talk for one or two minutes. Practise the vocabulary you have learnt so far in this unit.

> Describe a memorable holiday.
>
> You should say:
>
> > when you went on this holiday
> >
> > where you went
> >
> > what you did
>
> and explain why it is memorable.

Now listen to the sample answer.

Pronunciation: Extra stress

Sometimes we need to give a word extra stress. We can also stress a function word or a syllable that is normally unstressed. We may do this:

- to emphasise something
- to contrast two ideas/points/viewpoints, etc.
- to correct/disagree with someone.

10 1 For each sentence a–d, underline the word(s) that you think is/are given extra stress.

   a   I wanted to go but I couldn't. I was broke.
   b   Did you say her name was Julie? – No, Julia.
   c   My husband really enjoyed the mini break, but I didn't.
   d   Was your purse on the table when it was stolen? – No, it was under the table.

48
CD2

   2 Listen and check your answers. Then practise saying the sentences with the extra stresses.

49
CD2

11 Listen to the four sentences. Correct the speaker, using extra stress as appropriate.

Example: I gather you're from New Zealand. – No, I'm not. I'm from BELgium.

12 **1** Another way we place extra emphasis on something in English is by adding *do/ does/did* to affirmative sentences in the present simple and past simple. Doing this expresses a contrast or a strong feeling. Listen as you read the examples.

*I **do** think it is unfair that we visit these countries without a thought for what impact tourism has on the local population.* (a strong feeling)

*I **do** like travelling abroad but I also don't mind spending my holidays relaxing at home.* (a contrast)

2 Add *do/does/did* to the following sentences, changing the verb as appropriate.

   a Although it's more expensive, many people go abroad for their holidays.

   b We nearly decided not to go to South Africa, but in the end we went.

   c I love being able to lie in when I'm on holiday.

3 Listen to check your answers. Then repeat the sentences, making sure to give extra stress to *do/does/did*.

> **Exam tip:** Be careful: if you overuse *do/does/did* for emphasis, it may appear that you don't know how to form the tenses correctly.

Language: Cause and effect

13 **1** Underline the phrases used to link the cause and effect in sentences 1–6 below.

   a People have more disposable income than previous generations, which means that most people can now afford to go on holiday.

   b The rapid rise in air travel stems from the creation of low-cost airlines.

   c Competition between airlines has led to lower prices for passengers.

   d Staff working for our national airline keep striking. As a result, many people avoid booking with them.

   e I suffer from seasickness so I never travel by boat.

   f The severe delays were brought about by the volcanic eruption.

2 Now identify each cause and effect.

3 Talk about the effects of tourism from Exercise 3 on page 89, and any ideas of your own, using the cause-and-effect phrases you have learnt.

IELTS Speaking Exam: Part 3

14 You are going to hear some questions that are typical of Part 3 of the exam. Answer the questions, putting the language you have learnt in this unit into practice.

Now listen to the sample answers.

> **Exam tip:** Don't be afraid to express strong opinions in the exam. As you can see from the sample answers, it is appropriate to give strong opinions as long as you say nothing offensive. Expressing such views will make the discussion you have with the examiner more engaging.

Exam technique: What kind of speaker are you?

Ascertaining what kind of speaker you are will show you what to focus on during your revision. It will also help you maximise your performance in the exam.

1   **Choose the answers that best describe you (be honest!). If possible, also ask a friend and a teacher if they agree with you.**

  1   When I speak English,
  - a   I want to be as accurate as possible.
  - b   I tend just to think about communicating my message – I love talking.
  - c   I am able to focus equally on accuracy and communicating my message.

  2   Thinking about grammar,
  - a   I always try to use the new grammar I have learnt, though I may not always be accurate.
  - b   I use only the grammar I know well because I prefer not to make mistakes.
  - c   I am confident with grammar – I know the basics and more complex grammar and can use it all accurately.

  3   Thinking about vocabulary,
  - a   I know which words are formal and informal, and use them correctly; I also try to use less common words and idioms to show I have a wide vocabulary; I realise that collocations are important and I try to use them.
  - b   I don't think I have a wide vocabulary – I often repeat words and I mainly use common words like *good*, *interesting*, and *like*.
  - c   I can talk comfortably and well on familiar topics like *family* and *hobbies*, but I find it difficult to talk on unfamiliar topics.

  4   When it comes to pronunciation,
  - a   I don't really think about it.
  - b   I think I have almost native-like pronunciation.
  - c   I wish my pronunciation was much better.

  5   Thinking especially about Part 2,
  - a   I can rarely talk for two minutes on a topic.
  - b   I can sometimes talk for two minutes but I think I repeat myself a bit.
  - c   I have no trouble talking for two minutes.

2   **Now read the advice for the answers you chose.**

  1   a   If you are so worried about accuracy that you speak slowly and hesitate often, this will impact every aspect of your performance in the exam. Practise speaking as much as possible to increase your confidence. It is good to work on your accuracy before the exam, but in the exam, do not worry about accuracy and try to speak freely.
  - b   You may score well for fluency, but might score less well for grammatical accuracy and pronunciation. Record yourself and listen carefully to the mistakes you make, then re-record yourself trying to answer more accurately.
  - c   You will probably score well for accuracy, pronunciation and fluency. Make sure you are aware of any faults you have so you know what to improve.

2 a You are doing the right thing by attempting to use new and more complex grammar. However, ensure that you make few mistakes with more basic grammar.

b To achieve a high mark, you must attempt a range of complex grammar. You do not always have to use complex grammar correctly, but you must attempt it.

c You will probably achieve high marks for grammatical range and accuracy. Make sure you keep pushing yourself to use new structures.

3 a You will probably score well for lexical resource. Continue to note down new vocabulary, including collocations, and make sure you can use it appropriately.

b Read the sample answers and newspaper articles, noting down any new vocabulary (single words and collocations). Memorise it and test yourself frequently. Practise answering the exam questions using your new vocabulary.

c Write a list of at least ten 'difficult' topics. Use the sample answers and newspaper articles to find and learn vocabulary on these topics. Then practise talking about them, giving your opinion, and talking about the topic in relation to your country and experiences.

4 a You must think about it, as pronunciation represents a quarter of your mark in the exam and will also affect your marks for fluency. Record yourself answering an exam question and listen to your pronunciation. Ask a friend and/or teacher to listen, too. Check all the pronunciation points in this book, and score yourself on each one, e.g. word stress, and linking. Study again the ones that need the most improvement and practise speaking, focusing on these pronunciation points, one at a time.

b If a friend and/or teacher agree with you, you will probably score well for pronunciation. Do you use more complex features, such as linking and the schwa?

c Maybe your pronunciation is not as bad as you think. It doesn't matter if you have a foreign accent, as long as people can understand you without making special effort. Ask friends, preferably with a different mother tongue, or a teacher to tell you honestly what they think of your pronunciation. Study the pronunciation points in this book again. In addition, listen to the native speakers on the CD accompanying the book, pause the CD after each sentence and repeat what they say, focusing only on your pronunciation.

5 a Read the Part 2 sample answers aloud. See how the speaker expands on the sub-topics, giving details and personal responses, etc. Then record yourself answering the same questions – where could you expand your answer? Think about what else you could say and make some notes. Then try speaking for two minutes again.

b Record yourself answering a Part 2 question and then practise elaborating more in each part of your answer. What more relevant detail could you add? Find synonyms for words and expressions you have overused and learn them.

c Is everything you say relevant to the question? Does what you say have structure (with logical sequencing and a clear beginning, middle and end)? The examiner must be able to follow your speech easily.

12 Practice exam

You are going to do a practice exam. Listen to Tracks 57 to 60, and answer the examiner's questions. You may want to record yourself.

Note that, in Part 2 of the real exam, after you have talked for one to two minutes, the examiner will ask you one or two questions on the same topic. This is demonstrated in the sample answer.

Note also that Part 3 is a two-way discussion between you and the examiner. Of course, this cannot be replicated exactly with recorded questions, but you can see how this works by studying the sample answer.

PART 1: Introduction and interview (4–5 minutes)

53
CD2

Listen to Track 53, pausing the CD after each question to answer.

PART 2: Individual long turn (3–4 minutes)

54
CD2

Before you read the task card, listen to Track 54.

> Describe a personal achievement you are proud of.
>
> You should say:
>
> > what you achieved
> >
> > when you achieved it
> >
> > what was difficult about achieving it
>
> and explain why you are proud of this achievement.

You will have to talk about the topic for one to two minutes.
You have one minute to think about what you are going to say.
You can make some notes to help you if you wish.

Give yourself exactly one minute to think about your answer. Then listen to Track 55 before you begin speaking.

55
CD2

PART 3: Two-way discussion (4–5 minutes)

56
CD2

Listen to Track 56, pausing the CD after each question to answer.

Listen to Track 57 to hear a sample answer.

57
CD2

Audio scripts

Track 01

1   The person I'm closest to in my family is definitely my mum, Kate. We've always got on and we hardly ever fall out. I know that's unusual! She's really outgoing and sociable – she's always going out with friends and colleagues. Everyone thinks she's good fun. I look up to her because she's so hard working – she never sits still and she works long hours. She can be a bit impatient, though – she gets annoyed when her colleagues aren't as efficient as her. I take after her in that – I'm impatient, too. And she's over-sensitive, often getting offended for seemingly no reason.

2   My cousin Kieron and I grew up together. We were inseparable. He was so creative – he'd always think of new games we could play and make up these stories to make me laugh. I was constantly amazed by his open-mindedness as well – he was never judgemental. I wish I could be like that. Unfortunately, we grew apart, slowly but surely, and by the time we went to uni we weren't in touch any more. I haven't seen him for years. It's really sad. I would blame it partly on the fact that he's not very reliable, so for example, if I email him he won't respond. I'm not sure what he's up to these days.

3   I know this is a cliché, but I don't get on with my in-laws, especially my mother-in-law, Jane. She's so nosy, always wanting to know what we're doing and who we're with, and she's terribly blunt, which means she quite often upsets us with things she comes out with. And then she can be quite stingy. When we go out for a meal with her and my father-in-law, she never offers to pay, even though they're much better off than us. I must say, though, she's extremely clever and I do respect her for that. She set up her own business five years ago and it's gone from strength to strength. She's so self-assured and ambitious too, which I suppose is why she's so successful in business.

Track 02

Tell me something about your family.
What do you like doing most with your family?
Who are you close to in your family?
In what way is your family important to you?

Sample answers:

Examiner:	Tell me something about your family.
Candidate:	Although I live abroad now, my mum's family is from Paris and my dad's family is from Toulouse. So I'm from a very French family. I would say I come from quite a small family, really. For example, I just have one older sister and four cousins, but it's true that my extended family is fairly big.
Examiner:	What do you like doing most with your family?
Candidate:	I like having nice long meals with good food and good wine, and a few jokes for dessert!
Examiner:	Who are you close to in your family?
Candidate:	In my family? Well, I'm close to my Uncle Jacques. He's a chef. He's hilarious, always telling jokes, and he's very enthusiastic about everything he does. We spent a lot of time together when I was growing up. In fact he helped to bring me up.
Examiner:	In what way is your family important to you?
Candidate:	My family is everything to me. They are my best friends, they support me when things aren't going well and when things *are* going well. I know they'll always be there for me, no matter what.

Track 03

Candidate: One of my best friends is a guy called Raúl. I met him at uni in Barcelona where we were in the same study group. When was that? I suppose it was over 10 years ago now, so, yes, we've known each other for a good decade. We got to know each other on the tennis courts because the first few days of our course were so boring that we both decided we'd be better off outside playing tennis.

What kind of person is he? He's very active, a sporty type, involved in hiking and mountain biking – a bit of an adrenalin junky. He's also a very determined person. When he gets into something, he gives one hundred per cent. And he changes passions often. That makes him a bit of a self-absorbed person actually, which I'd say is a drawback. And I think he comes across as full of himself sometimes; I mean a bit too sure of his own opinions! As for why I like him, well, he's actually quite different from me. At uni, he'd often suggest doing something and I'd go along with it, and because I'm laid back I never felt overwhelmed by him. We've never fallen out or anything.

Examiner: How often do you see your friend?

Candidate: Well, because we live in different countries, we don't see each other that often, but we try to catch up on a fairly regular basis, say three times a year.

Tracks 04–06

See pages 12–13 for text.

Track 07

Modern families

In what ways have families changed in the last hundred years?
Should we rely heavily on our families or is it better to try to be independent?
The elderly are sometimes considered the wisest members of society. What do you think we can learn from them?

Friendship

What do you expect from a good friend?
Are friends as important to you as family?
Do you think friendships change as we get older? How?

Sample answers:

Examiner: In what ways have families changed in the last hundred years?

Candidate: In Western countries, I would say families have become more widely dispersed and less close. People travel more, and then end up living far from their families. I think this is a shame because it means there is a breakdown of communities. I also think that because families are spread over a wider geographical area, elderly people tend to be forgotten and usually live on their own.

Examiner: Should we rely heavily on our families or is it better to try to be independent?

Candidate: People seem to like living independently from each other these days, but I do wonder if that's the best way. Relying on people is seen as a weakness by some, I think. However, having family nearby is invaluable when you have children, in my opinion. Who else can be called on to babysit at a moment's notice?

Examiner: The elderly are sometimes considered the wisest members of society. What do you think we can learn from them?

Candidate:	Oh, an immense amount! They're our living link with the past – of a family, a region, a country. They're the keepers of local traditions, for example, and they provide a sense of identity to younger generations. It often seems to me that older people had harder lives and lived through more interesting periods in history, so I always enjoy asking my grandparents about their childhoods and how things have changed. Also, because they've got more life experience, older people are very well placed to give good advice on, well, any topic.
Examiner:	What do you expect from a good friend?
Candidate:	For me, a good friend has to be reliable. I can't stand being stood up or having my emails and texts ignored. As well as that, a friend should be someone you can have good fun with. There are many things in life to be serious about, but friendship shouldn't be one of them. I also believe that opposites attract, in friendships just as in romance, so a good friend will most likely be very different from you in many ways.
Examiner:	Are friends as important to you as family?
Candidate:	No, I wouldn't say so. Friends come and go, but family are always there, whether you like it or not. You can even be rude to your family – not that it's advisable, of course! – and they will forgive you. But sometimes you've known a friend for so long they can become like a family member – you can really be yourself with them and you may even argue quite often, like siblings do.
Examiner:	Do you think friendships change as we get older?
Candidate:	Well, I definitely find that I have less in common with some friends than I used to. I sometimes wonder what we used to find to talk about. And so you often grow apart from old school friends or old colleagues. The people I feel I have most in common with are friends I met at university. I'm not sure why but we somehow always have lots to talk about.

Track 08

It's by far my favourite sport to watch. I love the excitement that builds up as the match progresses, with the fans cheering and chanting. There's always an amazing atmosphere.

My team usually loses, it has to be said, although last week they drew. When they play away I always try to go and support them. And I've got the latest kit, but they're getting more and more expensive so I may have to stop buying them. I think the clubs take advantage of fans' loyalty to push up the prices.

Team sports are a fantastic way for young people to improve their fitness. I coach a junior team at the weekend. We don't train in a stadium, of course, just on a pitch in our local park. I was really delighted last week when our youngest player scored the winning goal with a beautiful header. I think he might prove to be a real up-and-coming talent.

Track 09

What do you do to keep fit?
Are you good at sport?
What sports do you play?
What is the most popular sport in your country?

Sample answers:	
Examiner:	What do you do to keep fit?
Candidate:	I go to the gym twice a week. I don't really enjoy it, to be honest, but it's an easy way to keep fit. I mainly do cardiovascular exercises, rather than muscle building.
Examiner:	Are you good at sport?
Candidate:	Not really, but I try my best. I prefer individual sports to team sports because if I do badly in a team game I always feel I'm letting everyone down.

Examiner:	What sports do you play?
Candidate:	I go kite-surfing sometimes. I enjoy it because it's so exhilarating. I can't go often, though, because there's rarely enough wind where I live. I might take up another water sport instead.
Examiner:	What is the most popular sport in your country?
Candidate:	I'd say the most popular sport is football, as in most countries. Most people have a favourite team who they support through thick and thin. The teams are often English ones, and Manchester United is the most well-known.

Track 10

Speaker 1:	Oh great, the match is starting!
Speaker 2:	Oh great, the match is starting.
Speaker 3:	Liverpool won. Fantastic.
Speaker 4:	Liverpool won! Fantastic!

Tracks 11–12

See page 20 for text.

Track 13

Candidate: I'd like to talk about the most exciting tennis match I've ever seen. It was about six years ago just outside Bordeaux in France, and it was the boys' final of a junior championship. My favourite player, a rising star, had got to the final so I wanted to see him. At the time, I didn't know anyone else who was interested in tennis – all my friends preferred football – so I went on my own. I set off really early to make sure I got there on time, but I ended up being too early and I had to wait for two hours for the match to start. It didn't matter, though, because this meant I got one of the best seats, right at the front in the middle of the court – I was delighted about that.

Other people gradually started arriving, the seats filled up, and we waited expectantly for the players. When the match started, it soon became clear that I was practically the only person supporting Jean Martin. Most people were there to support the other guy who had won the previous two years and was the favourite to win this year, too. Every time Paul Fernandez won a point, the crowd erupted into applause but I sat silently, getting more and more anxious. Martin lost the first set, but then there was a dramatic turnaround. He suddenly seemed to find some self-belief and he started to win. That's what I love about tennis – it's a battle of the mind as much as the body. I find it interesting to see how some players may be highly skilled but don't have the mental strength to win. Martin obviously did have this strength, and Fernandez was slowly falling apart. The atmosphere was electric. Martin showed off his amazing skills, hitting ball after ball straight down the line. Martin served for the match – you could have heard a pin drop. When he served an ace, the crowd went wild! Although they had begun by supporting his opponent, they had grown to respect him for his cool head and control of the ball. When he was presented with the trophy, he cried with joy.

Examiner:	Do you play tennis yourself?
Candidate:	Yes, I'm a keen tennis player. I joined a club about two years ago and play all the time.

Track 14

Keeping fit

What are the best ways to keep fit?
Do you think most people consider exercise a chore or do they find it fun?
What is the most popular form of exercise in your country?

Healthy lifestyles

Do you think people in your country are less healthy than they used to be?
How can we encourage young people to stay healthy?
Should governments intervene to force people to be healthier?

Sample answers:

Keeping fit

Examiner: What are the best ways to keep fit?

Candidate: The best way to keep fit is to do exercise that raises your heart rate. The heart is a muscle and has to be worked like any other muscle. So golf, in my opinion, is not the best form of exercise. Something like jogging or swimming or surfing is much more beneficial.

Examiner: Do you think most people consider exercise a chore or do they find it fun?

Candidate: I think most people feel it is something they *should* do. That is a mistake, as far as I'm concerned, because the best way to exercise is not to think about the fitness aspect and just have fun. You can exercise without even noticing you're doing it if you play volleyball with your friends, or go snorkelling, or go for a long walk on a sunny day, or something like that.

Examiner: What is the most popular form of exercise in your country?

Candidate: I would say the most popular form of exercise is going to the gym. I'm in two minds about the gym as a way to keep fit. On the one hand, it is convenient. But on the other hand, a gym is a very controlled environment, somewhat lacking in imagination and spontaneity.

Healthy lifestyles

Examiner: Do you think people in your country are less healthy than they used to be?

Candidate: Yes, definitely. I would argue that the invention of TV has led to people being much too sedentary. I know some people who refuse to have a television because they think that without one they are much more likely to keep active – it's all too easy to become a coach potato. Also, most people work in offices so they just sit in a chair all day long and only move to go to the photocopier. That's very unhealthy. People used to work the land and so be on the go from morning till night. Obesity was unknown then, except among the super rich, I imagine.

Examiner: How can we encourage young people to stay healthy?

Candidate: Parents should set a good example. But I strongly believe that schools have a crucial role to play. Not only can they offer a wide range of sports for children to play, they can teach them about eating a balanced diet, and the negative effects of eating junk food and not exercising. If children don't hear all this from home, they have to hear it from somewhere, and I would argue that it's the schools' responsibility. Once they get a taste for playing sports, they will love the sense of achievement it can give you and the feeling of camaraderie with your team mates, and then hopefully they won't ever want to stop playing sports.

Examiner: Should governments intervene to force people to be healthier?

Candidate: Hmm, I'm highly sceptical of the idea that governments should force their citizens to be healthy. People ought to be encouraged to lead healthy lives, but not forced to. They could, for example, run an ad campaign showing people how to eat a balanced diet – that you need to eat some carbohydrates, some vegetables and fruit, some meat and so on. I think most people don't know that. But I'm unconvinced that trying to force people into healthy habits would work because when bullied like that people tend to resent it and react by sticking even more firmly with their unhealthy lifestyles. The one area where I strongly believe legislation is necessary is with smoking. Smokers can harm others through passive smoking so they should not be allowed to smoke in public places. In fact, this has just recently been outlawed in my country.

Track 15

My name's Mubarak and I'm from the United Arab Emirates. My favourite subject at school was Maths. I really loved it, I think primarily because I liked being able to use logic to work out answers, rather than having to speculate and theorise, as you often do in arts subjects.

I went on to study for Bachelor's and Master's degrees, both in Mechanical Engineering at Leeds University in England. I chose that subject because, although I was more keen on Maths, engineering is more practical. My decision to study in Britain was motivated by the high prestige of British qualifications back in my home country. The tuition fees are very high for foreign students but my family paid them for me.

I found the course very challenging. English is, of course, not my mother tongue so I found some of the lectures and seminars hard to follow. As a result, I failed my first year exams. I had to retake them all, but then, thankfully, I passed. I always did well in my coursework because I could take time to research the topic and check my English.

My dream job would be to work as a mechanical engineer for the United Arab Emirates' Army. The reasons are that such a job carries high prestige, it would be interesting, and there would be good job security – if I got such a job, I would probably have it for life.

Track 16

Do you work or are you a student?
Why did you choose that course or job?
What is the most difficult thing about your studies or job?

Sample answers:

Examiner:	Do you work or are you a student?
Candidate:	I've just finished secondary school. I got the best results in my year so I'm hoping to get a scholarship to study English Literature.
Examiner:	Why did you choose that course?
Candidate:	Because I love literature. I love getting lost in a book; I mean, it's a form of escapism for me. But I also enjoy learning about the historical and cultural contexts that influenced a work and I'll have ample opportunity to learn about these things at university.
Examiner:	What was the most difficult thing about your studies?
Candidate:	At secondary school, the most difficult subject for me was Chemistry. I can't stand Science, and I would dread every lesson! I struggled in Chemistry lessons, and I had to work really hard to pass my exam. For some reason, I just couldn't remember all those chemical symbols and equations no matter how long I spent revising.

Track 17

Candidate: My dream job would be to teach children to sail. I have some qualifications, in skippering, for example, but it's very likely I would need more, such as a teaching certificate from the Yachting Association. I have some of the right experience in that I've been sailing a long time – I'm confident in handling a yacht and I've dealt with many minor crises in my time, like getting trapped in storms and saving someone who'd fallen overboard. It's true that I've never taught anyone but I don't think that would be a problem, provided I was given adequate training – I'm quite good with people and can explain things clearly. I imagine the job would involve encouraging youngsters to try sailing for the first time; and also teaching them that by working together as a team they could discover they have hidden strengths. The most difficult thing would be having sufficient patience when the children didn't do as they were told. I suspect it would be frustrating if they didn't realise that the rules were there for their own safety. Why is it my dream job? It's my dream job because I love sailing – it's been my hobby for decades. And I'd like to work in a nice, warm climate where all I'd need to worry about was making sure I had suntan lotion on and enough to drink.

Examiner: When did you learn to sail?

Candidate: I learnt when I was a small boy. My dad taught me as he was a very skilled sailor. He taught my brothers and sister, too, and we're all very pleased he did.

Track 18

Education

Do you think science subjects are more useful than arts subjects?

Are students mature enough to choose what to study themselves or should their parents decide for them?

In your country, does having a university education help you into a better career?

Motivation

Do you think older or younger workers are more motivated?

How can managers increase motivation among their workforce?

Are people more motivated if their job involves helping others?

Sample answers:

Education

Examiner: Do you think science subjects are more useful than arts subjects?

Candidate: I think they *are* more useful because they are primarily concerned with practical matters. If you study science, you might, for example, go on to have some kind of technical role in the production of a device, like a computer or a car. However, all great leaders have studied more arty subjects, such as philosophy, history and economics. This makes them better leaders because they have an understanding of human nature.

Examiner: Are young people mature enough to choose what to study themselves or should their parents decide for them?

Candidate: I think success in studying comes from being highly motivated to study a specific subject area. Therefore the student should choose which subject they're interested in. By way of an example, I had a friend who studied science A levels because his parents pushed him down that route, but he hated it and so didn't get very good results. He still graduated and managed to get a place at university where he studied law, and he became a top student because law was what he was interested in.

Examiner: In your country, does having a university education help you into a better career?

Candidate: Yes, it does, as all top companies recruit graduates for their top positions. Therefore you get a better start. However, it's fair to say that a university degree is not everything and it's what you do with it that matters. You can have a degree yet still get overtaken by somebody who isn't university educated but who gets promoted over you because they work harder.

Motivation

Examiner: Do you think older or younger workers are more motivated?

Candidate: Younger workers should be more motivated because everything in their job is new to them and therefore exciting and they have to build their career, which is all ahead of them. Older workers have a tendency to think they've seen it all and very often just wait for retirement. I do know of at least one older person who's made a point of retiring on a high and is therefore highly motivated to get a project delivered to a very high standard before he retires. But no matter how fascinating your job is, when you reach the end of your career, I suspect you mainly focus on your impending retirement.

Examiner: How can managers increase motivation among their workforce?

Candidate: Allocating the right tasks to the person with the right skills, but making every task slightly different so that they learn every time. That can lead to an increase in motivation. It's about making the job interesting, but without drowning staff in too much new information each time. If they see that they can progress steadily and meet the challenges set, then they'll stay motivated.

Examiner: Are people more motivated if their job involves helping others?

Candidate: Although my job doesn't really involve helping people, just training them, I'd hazard a guess that youth workers, for example, find it very rewarding helping a young person to achieve their personal goals or overcome a personal challenge. I can imagine, too, that it gives a counsellor tremendous job satisfaction to know that if they weren't there to listen to their patients' problems, things would probably not turn out as well for them. So, yes, although it's impossible for me to know for sure, I'd say people with those kinds of jobs take more pleasure from their work and are motivated by something more profound than just money.

Tracks 19–20

See pages 29–30 for text.

Track 21

Speaker 1: Where I come from it's almost always sweltering. Ours is an arid climate, and in most parts of the country precipitation is very low. Can you believe that in the summer, the temperature can exceed 50°C?

Speaker 2: Sometimes I feel like it's constantly drizzling here and it generally feels damp. In fact, right now it's pouring down. That does mean we have the most beautiful lush, green countryside, though. And the climate is temperate, so we don't suffer from any extreme weather, thank goodness.

Speaker 3: The weather here is notoriously changeable. People often think our country is very, very cold all the time, but ocean currents keep our climate fairly mild, considering the latitude. I don't mind our winters, which are bearable as long as you wrap up warm, but I don't like our summers because it never gets above 25°C.

Track 22

Tell me about your country's climate.
What's your favourite kind of weather?
Does the weather influence your mood?
Is it worse to feel too hot or too cold?

Track 23

Examiner: Tell me about your country's climate.

Candidate: We have an extreme climate. Our winters are absolutely freezing, and our summers are boiling hot. That means that the people, the houses, the transport system, everything needs to be prepared to cope with every kind of weather.

Examiner: What's your favourite kind of weather?

Candidate: What I like most is hot, dry weather. I love being able to sit outside on a balmy evening with a drink, rather than cooped up inside like you are in the winter.

Examiner: Does the weather influence your mood?

Candidate: Yes, it certainly does. It's the rain that influences my mood the most. I hate it when it's raining – it makes me feel so down. It's hard to go out, without getting soaked to the skin, anyway. And the sky is so dismal and overcast. It's miserable!

Examiner: Is it worse to feel too hot or too cold?

Candidate: Well, I suppose if it's too cold you can just wear more layers, but nevertheless I prefer to be too hot. At least it means the weather is good, and you can always go for a swim to cool down. What I really can't stand is being cold and wet. That's the worst combination and it makes me worry that I'm going to catch a cold.

Track 24

Candidate: My favourite season is most certainly the summer, which is officially from June to September. I say 'officially' because the reality is that we generally get a very short summer, in that the weather is only really 'summery' for a few weeks a year. The rest of the season merges with the others, being rather cold and rainy. The highest the temperature gets is about 30, and when it gets that high, people start complaining because they're not used to such heat. This irritates me, to be honest, because my view is that we so rarely have hot weather that we should just appreciate it and enjoy it when we do. In this country, and especially in my region, you can't rely on good weather in the summer. I've been to many outdoor events, like weddings, concerts, barbecues and so on, where the organisers were optimistic about the weather, but where it rained non-stop. Of course, you can't blame them – if you can't organise an outdoor event in August, when can you?

In the summer, I typically go abroad on holiday to places where scorching sunshine is practically guaranteed. This is because I am a sun worshipper and like to get a good tan. Having sun on my skin makes me feel healthy, though I am fully aware of all the dangers associated with too much exposure to the sun. When I am at home, I like to have friends over for barbecues, and we stay out in the garden all evening until it gets too chilly or until it's time for them to go home.

The reason summer is my favourite season is that sunshine makes me happy. It's a scientific fact that it releases endorphins. In fact, during the winter many people in my country use light boxes, which recreate the light of the sun. You have to sit and stare into the light and it is intended to lift your mood. In the summer, though, you don't need such gadgets; you can just go outside, sit in the sun and get a natural energy boost. It's wonderful.

Examiner: Do you dislike the winter?

Candidate: No, I don't. All the seasons have something to offer. In the winter it's nice to snuggle up inside, with a mug of hot chocolate.

Tracks 25–28

See pages 37–38 for text

Track 29

The environment

Are people in your country concerned about protecting the environment?

Does the responsibility for protecting the environment lie with governments or with individuals?

Does it help to educate young people on being green?

Pollution

What effects does pollution have on the environment?
Do you think we pollute more now than we did 50 years ago?
What do you think will happen if we do not reduce current levels of pollution?

Sample answers:

The environment

Examiner: Are people in your country concerned about protecting the environment?

Candidate: To be honest, no. I think the middle and upper classes are more interested in earning as much money as they can in order to buy as much stuff as they can. And there are many people in my country who live below the poverty line and they quite literally can't afford to worry about the environment when they're struggling to put food on the table and just survive.

Examiner: Does the responsibility for protecting the environment lie with governments or with individuals?

Candidate: In my view, the responsibility lies with all of us. However, individuals, at least in my country, aren't taking action of their own accord, and nor are businesses; *they're* just out to make a profit. Therefore, it falls to governments to force people to be more green, for example by fining companies that release toxic waste into our rivers, or incentivising us to recycle.

Examiner: Does it help to educate young people on being green?

Candidate: Almost certainly it does, because it is the next generation who will have to take on the huge burden of saving the planet. This generation isn't doing enough and is too worried about money, so I pray that the next one will see the urgency of the situation, and the way to get them to see is to teach them about the repercussions of a polluting lifestyle such as ours.

Pollution

Examiner: What effects does pollution have on the environment?

Candidate: Oh, I hardly know where to start! Pollution in the oceans kills fish and so unbalances the ecosystem. Pollution on land means that whole areas become unfit to live on or to farm. Habitats are destroyed, which leads to the extinction of hundreds of animal and plant species.

Examiner: Do you think we pollute more now than we did fifty years ago?

Candidate: Well, yes, overall. I'd say, though, that richer countries pollute less themselves but export their pollution elsewhere, by which I mean that they consume foreign products that have a large carbon footprint. It has become fashionable to be green in wealthier nations, especially Western ones, so people make an effort to cycle to work and recycle their waste. However, it's quite a shallow attempt at being green, in my opinion, because they still live in big houses using lots of energy and go on holidays abroad, leaving a trail of pollution in their wake.

Examiner: What do you think will happen if we don't reduce current levels of pollution?

Candidate: I read an article recently that claimed if we don't change our ways, we will need a second planet to meet our needs as early as 2030. It's frightening to think that we're that greedy, and I'm sure I'm just as guilty as the next person. I do hold out some hope that things will get so bad that we will realise we really *must* act, and we will completely change our destructive habits just in the nick of time. If not, the planet will surely become uninhabitable.

Track 30

My mother tongue is Hungarian. It is spoken in Hungary and it is a minority language in the surrounding countries, especially Romania. It is not part of the same language family as European languages like English, French, German or Russian. It is a Uralic language, distantly related to Finnish and Estonian. Because Hungarian is not a widely spoken language, if you want to get on, you have to speak a foreign language. Unsurprisingly, the most popular second language among Hungarians is English, the global language. Like most of my friends, I am multilingual – as well as Hungarian, I am fluent in English and German. I can also get by in Italian and I did an evening course in Spanish a few years back, but I'm a bit rusty now. I seem to pick up languages quite easily, helped, I'm sure, by the fact that language teaching in Hungary is so good – it has to be, given that no-one speaks our language but us!

Track 31

What's your mother tongue?
What other languages do you speak?
What do you think is the best way to keep in touch with friends?
Do people keep in touch differently now compared to fifty years ago?

Sample answers:

Examiner:	What's your mother tongue?
Candidate:	My mother tongue is Portuguese. It's predominantly spoken in Brazil but also in other parts of the world, such as Portugal and Africa.
Examiner:	What other languages do you speak?
Candidate:	Although I grew up in Brazil, I can also speak Italian because my mother and one set of grandparents are Italian and I grew up hearing the language all around me. I'm really proud to be bilingual and I'd like my children to be bilingual too.
Examiner:	What do you think is the best way to keep in touch with friends?
Candidate:	It depends how far you are from your friends. If you are geographically close, you should meet up face-to-face. Long-distance communication can cause misunderstandings and resentments to build up – when you write, you only have the words on the page, not body language or tone of voice.
Examiner:	Do people keep in touch differently now compared to fifty years ago?
Candidate:	Well, of course, people use the Internet now and mobile phones. I'm quite young but even when I was a teenager nobody in my friendship circle had a mobile. Now it's seen as indispensible and you would feel left out if you didn't have one. But as I said before, I think it's better to meet up with friends than to communicate using technology. There's much to be said for communicating in so-called old-fashioned ways.

Track 32

Candidate: A language I would like to learn is Spanish. It's used not only in Spain but also in many other countries, and I believe it's one of the most widely-spoken languages in the world. So it's a language that is definitely worth knowing. It would be useful to me for business purposes. Also, Spanish culture is becoming more and more influential internationally. It is, for example, overtaking English as the most widely-spoken language in certain parts of the USA. It is influencing music and art. So, all in all, I think it's a handy language to know.

I doubt it would be too challenging for me to learn Spanish because it is a Latin language, just like my mother tongue, French. I think Spanish vocabulary would be easier for me to acquire than Spanish grammar. I understand the grammar is one of the most difficult things about the Spanish language.

I would use Spanish primarily when going on holiday. I've been to Spain many times, and I always find that if you go off the beaten track it's difficult to find people who speak English. You get very good at speaking with your hands! And it's difficult to really engage with people and understand the culture if you don't speak the language. Speaking Spanish would undoubtedly make my holidays a lot easier and more enjoyable. On top of that, the company I work for has an office in Madrid and it would also be very interesting to be able to work there. I would enjoy the challenge and the exposure to a new culture. It would be such an exciting opportunity. To make the move, though, I'd obviously need to be able to speak Spanish. Luckily, my company would most likely sponsor me to have Spanish lessons.

Examiner: Where have you been in Spain?

Candidate: I've been to Spain many times and each time I did a road trip. One trip was in the north of Spain, travelling from France across the Pyrenees, through the Basque country and all the way down to Madrid.

Track 33

See page 46 for text.

Track 34

1 sixth
2 strong
3 glimpsed
4 three

Track 35

Language learning

Is it considered important in your country to learn foreign languages?
What, in your opinion, is the best way to learn a language?
Why are some people seemingly better at learning languages than others?

English as a global language

How do people in your country feel about English being the world language?
Do you think the culture of English-speaking countries, as well as the English language, dominate the world?
Why do you think people feel it is important to continue speaking their local languages?

Sample answers:

Examiner: Is it considered important in your country to learn foreign languages?

Candidate: More than just important, it's considered essential. The English poet John Donne said 'no man is an island', and I think in this day and age that is also true of countries: we are all intricately connected. A country that wants to do business abroad and export its goods has to know how to communicate with foreigners, and that means speaking foreign languages.

Examiner: What, in your opinion, is the best way to learn a language?

Candidate: Undoubtedly, the best way is to go and live in a country where the language is spoken as a native language. But that is not enough – I have friends who have done just that, but they stuck together with people who spoke their language and so they hardly learnt anything. You have to immerse yourself completely in the language and the culture.

This takes courage but is well worth the effort. One of my friends went to study in England and got an English boyfriend. Her English improved dramatically in just a few months, so arguably that's the best way!

Examiner: Why are some people seemingly better at learning languages than others?

Candidate: It's true that some people seem to pick up language really easily. Being bilingual from a young age certainly helps because the more languages you speak, the more easily you acquire a new one. Another major factor is motivation: two people can study the same materials for the same number of hours but the person who is more motivated will learn more and remember better what they've learnt. I really believe that the more you *care* about learning a language, the more effortlessly you will pick it up.

Examiner: How do people in your country feel about English being the world language?

Candidate: I don't think most people *feel* anything exactly; they just see it as something inevitable. They don't fight it because that would just leave them trailing behind other countries that embrace English as the global lingua franca. Not learning English would leave us economically disadvantaged.

Examiner: Do you think the culture of English-speaking countries, as well as the English language, dominate the world?

Candidate: The rise of the Internet has certainly increased the dominance of English, and therefore also the spread of English and American ways of seeing the world. I think we are all expected to conform. Also, the majority of young people in my country like to watch American films and listen to American music: it's considered trendy to do so. So, yes, I would definitely say that the culture of English-speaking countries holds much sway all over the world.

Examiner: Why do you think people feel it is important to continue speaking their local languages?

Candidate: There is a backlash in some quarters against the spread of English. One way this is expressed is by the insistence on maintaining local languages. A local language is more than just words. It links a community with its past, with its heritage, and so if you stop speaking your language, you lose a part of yourself.

Track 36

Examiner: Which language do you think is generally considered the most beautiful?

Candidate: Well, I think Italian is generally considered the most beautiful European language. It's probably because of the, um, the music of the language, the way speakers sound like they're singing. Personally, er, I prefer Spanish.

Track 37

Examiner: So, everyone in your country speaks English?

Candidate: Actually, no they don't. It is primarily young people who learn English at school. The older generation tend to speak only our native language.

Examiner: American music is more popular than other forms of music, is it?

Candidate: Not exactly, no. Japanese music is also extremely popular.

Track 38

What do you use the Internet for?
Does everyone have access to the Internet in your country?
Do you think older people are scared of new technology?
Do you think young children should have mobile phones?

Sample answers:

Examiner: What do you use the Internet for?

Candidate: I mainly use the Internet to read newspapers and news items, mostly about sport. I also use it to do a bit of research on things to do and things to see at the weekends. I do a bit of internet shopping, like booking flights and accommodation for my holidays.

Examiner: Does everyone have access to the Internet in your country?

Candidate: I think so. Obviously, people in urban areas have wider access to the Internet. It's still a very rural country though, so, on second thoughts, I'm not sure that everybody is connected. And certainly not everyone has broadband.

Examiner: Do you think older people are scared of new technology?

Candidate: Some older people embrace new technology. My granddad, for example, was a technophile and wanted to keep up to speed with the latest technology. However, I would say that most older people don't bother learning about new technology simply because they can't see what it would bring to their lives.

Examiner: Do you think young children should have mobile phones?

Candidate: I can't see that young children have much use for mobile phones, at least in terms of using the phone as a phone. They might find it interesting to have a device to listen to music and take photos. But I can't imagine many young kids making calls.

Track 39

Candidate: The piece of equipment I'd like to talk about is my iPhone, which is a smartphone. It has various uses. It functions as a normal phone so you can make calls and text people. But, more unusually for a phone, you can also surf the Internet and send emails. It also acts as a camera, though admittedly not a very good one. You can buy applications from an online store, which allow you to find your way, play games, read e-books, and much more besides. New applications are being added all the time, and some of them are really crazy, like one that lets you record your voice and then it plays it back to you but making you sound like an alien! And last but not least, you can listen to your music and watch videos.

It was a present from my parents. I'd been pestering them for months to get me one and at last they gave in, when it came round to my birthday. I think they bought it online as it was cheaper that way. I was the first of my friends to get one, and I think they were all really envious. It is the latest must-have. People love it because it is so beautifully made, so intuitive, so robust and so clever.

It is because it is so many things rolled into one that it is so useful. I just love my iPhone, and if I lost it I wouldn't know what to do with myself. I use it on the way to university to entertain myself, I use it to stay in touch with my friends, I use it to check where I am. It's not so much useful to me as absolutely essential.

Examiner: What piece of electronic equipment would you not miss?

Candidate: That's a difficult question because I love gadgets and all things technological. If I had to choose something, I'd say kitchen gadgets.

Tracks 40–43

See pages 52–53 for text.

Track 44

Technological developments

What have been the most significant technological developments of recent years?
In what ways have these developments changed society for the better and for the worse?
Are people in your country nostalgic about life before technology?

Science and ethics

Why do you think some people claim scientists interfere too much with nature?
Do you have anything against animal testing?
Is scientific progress always for the greater good?

Sample answers:

Examiner: What have been the most significant technological developments of recent years?

Candidate: Undoubtedly, ones connected with the Internet. The Internet has created a global village where everyone can easily and cheaply contact almost anyone in the world, just to chat or to do business or to find love. It's a revolution, the like of which I don't think has been seen before. We have the Internet at home through our personal computers but also on the move through the use of smartphones and laptops, so wherever we are we have access to almost limitless sources of knowledge.

Examiner: In what ways have these developments changed society for the better and for the worse?

Candidate: Well, as I said, they have brought people closer together in many ways. However, there are disadvantages. First of all, some people believe everything they read online, which is dangerous. Then, many people spend too much time sitting in front of their computers rather than going out and socialising, so they put on weight, they don't develop and maintain friendship circles. Last but not least, it can cut dead debate. When I'm in the pub with my friends, we no longer have a friendly, informal debate about which band has sold the most albums. We just check our smartphones and find the answer in a few seconds, and then have nothing left to say to each other!

Examiner: Are people in your country nostalgic about life before technology?

Candidate: Yes, I think so, and not just the older generation. Younger people, too, are beginning to see that community is not what it was and that is largely due to technological developments. For example, before the car most people walked to work. This meant that they lived close to their place of work, and so everyone lived and worked in the same area and they all knew each other.

Examiner: Why do you think some people claim scientists interfere too much with nature?

Candidate: In my view, people are scared because scientists seem to be all-powerful. They come up with some new discovery almost every week. There seems to be no end to it. So people are bound to question whether it's right or not to delve so far into nature's secrets, manipulating genetic codes and so on. But then maybe progress is always scary and that's what keeps us interested. It is challenging and thought-provoking.

Examiner: Do you have anything against animal testing?

Candidate: I do if it's for the purposes of cosmetics and other unnecessary luxuries. I'm not sure what I think of testing on animals for reasons of finding cures for human illnesses. But I think it's something I'd rather not talk about, to be honest. I don't feel comfortable discussing it.

Examiner: Is scientific progress always for the greater good?

Candidate: Not necessarily. After all, scientists developed the atom bomb and all the efficient new ways we have of killing each other. What matters is that we keep on questioning scientists, letting them know that we are grateful for their discoveries but will not give them free rein. They need to keep morality in mind when they're working.

Track 45

What would you say were the advantages of having a mobile phone?

Track 46

Technology brings people closer together, for example by allowing friends on opposite sides of the world to chat to each other online. But then again, it can isolate people, for example if someone spends hours in front of their computer alone.

Track 47

What do you think of online shopping?

Track 48

My friend Kate and her mum went to see a movie in 3D for the first time the other night. She really enjoyed it.

Track 49

People from my country are very enthusiastic about technological advances. **People from my country** often go straight out and buy the latest gadget as soon as it's available in the shops. To be honest, I think **people from my country** are a bit materialistic and like to show off with their possessions.

In Britain, we are very enthusiastic about technological advances. **We** often go straight out and buy the latest gadget as soon as it's available in the shops. To be honest, I think **we** are a bit materialistic and like to show off our possessions.

Track 50

What do people in your country think of new technology?

Track 51

What are your hobbies?
What is your favourite musical instrument?
Do you prefer action films or comedies? Why?
Do you think it is important to read novels and poetry? Why?

Sample answers:

Examiner:	What are your hobbies?
Candidate:	There is no one thing I'm fanatical about. I have various interests. I'm a keen cook and love to create new dishes and then invite my friends over to taste them. I love playing cards, especially Uno. Most of my friends are crazy about karaoke and I go with them from time to time but it's not really my kind of thing.
Examiner:	What is your favourite musical instrument?
Candidate:	What is my favourite instrument? I would have to say the piano. I'm not a big classical music fan on the whole but I do love a bit of piano. It's the emotion it can express that fascinates me, the way man and instrument become one and the pianist gets lost in the music.
Examiner:	Do you prefer action films or comedies?
Candidate:	Neither really. If I had to choose between them I'd pick comedies, but what I really like is horror films, especially those involving ghosts. I enjoy getting a good fright.

Examiner: Do you think it is important to read novels and poetry?

Candidate: Well, my teachers always told me it is. But reading, I can take it or leave it. I can't remember the last time I picked up a real page-turner. I don't think it's important to read. You can be entertained by films and you can be educated via the television, watching documentaries and so on. So, I don't feel I'm missing out on anything.

Track 52

Sample answers:

Candidate: One of my favourite hobbies is going shopping. I've always loved it. I think I get it from my mum, who used to take me to the nearest town every weekend to visit shops and boutiques. She taught me about buying a few quality items that you may pay a premium for but that last a long time so are a good investment. She also taught me about how to check for the quality of a garment by looking at the way it's sewn together and also creasing the fabric to see if it stays creased or not. If it stays creased then it's a poor quality fabric. Another thing I learnt from her is how to find a bargain. You need to shop around and not be afraid of trying the smaller boutiques where you're more likely to find a shop owner who's happy to offer a discount. I've been shopping on my own since I was a student. Then, I could not afford to buy many things but stuck to what my mum taught me and kept my eyes open for a quality bargain. The rest of the time, I would window shop. Nowadays I can afford designer clothes but I still love the sales, when I hunt for a bargain and the odd top-designer item. One thing I hate, however, is trying things on because there are always long queues and it means you have less time for shopping. It's not a problem, not trying things on, because if something is not the right size I can take it back to the shop as long as I've kept the receipt.

   I go shopping every week. I find it therapeutic. It always makes you feel good to get your hands on a nice quality piece at a bargain price, and if I'm feeling a bit down there's nothing like a bit of retail therapy. I find shopping exciting as well. You spend time in the poshest part of town where you can mix with fashionable people. There's a buzz and it's busy and noisy and colourful. Shopping lets you keep up to speed with the latest trends. So all in all, I think it has a lot of benefits and I love it.

Examiner: What's the best bargain you've ever got?

Candidate: I once bought a designer coat, 100% cashmere, absolutely beautiful, for 25% of the full price. It was in a closing-down sale.

CD 2

Track 01

1 How long have you lived here?
2 Have you ever eaten Italian food?
3 What has happened in the news today?
4 What have you done so far today?

Track 02

1   I've played the clarinet since I was a child. OR
    I've been playing the clarinet since I was a child.
2   I've only been scuba-diving twice.
3   I've known her for three and a half years.
4   I've read your book. You can have it back now.
5   I've been watching TV all morning. I'm so lazy!

Track 03

1   How long have you been doing your favourite hobby?
2   How many times have you engaged in your hobby this week, or this year?
3   Have you had less time for your hobby since you started studying for IELTS?

Track 04

Hobbies

Do you think men and women tend to have different types of hobbies?
Why do some people get obsessed with their hobby?
Do you think hobbies that keep you fit are better than hobbies that you can do sitting down?

Free time

Do you think it can be a disadvantage to have too much free time?
Should people feel a duty to do something constructive in their free time?
Do people have more free time now than in the past?

Sample answers:

Examiner: Do you think men and women tend to have different types of hobbies?

Candidate: Yes, I do. The men I know have sports as hobbies. The women usually enjoy more sedentary and peaceful hobbies, like reading or crafts. Having said that, there are of course women who love exhilarating hobbies or are fanatical about cycling or something. And there are men who take up pottery or sewing. There are always exceptions to every rule.

Examiner: Why do some people get obsessed with their hobby?

Candidate: I think everybody finds at least one thing absolutely fascinating. It can be anything – subjects like history of art, or a sport like basketball, or a craft like card-making. Everyone is different and one person's interest can appear strange to other people. However, not everyone has time to indulge themselves with their hobby. Mothers of young children, for example, get little free time and so they appear less 'obsessed' than a single man who spends every weekend, all weekend playing computer games.

Examiner: Do you think hobbies that keep you fit are better than hobbies that you can do sitting down?

Candidate: No, I think hobbies that open you up to new things are the best, ones that enrich you and give you a new skill. That can be anything, but it is important always to grow as a person and not become boring by never trying anything new.

Examiner: Do you think it can be a disadvantage to have too much free time?

Candidate: Well, they say that the devil makes work for idle hands and I think it's true that the less you have to do the less active you become and the more time you waste. People who have too much time to spare tend to become lazy and lethargic. People who are always on the go, on the other hand, think nothing of fitting one more thing into their busy schedules.

Examiner:	Should people feel a duty to do something constructive in their free time?
Candidate:	No, not necessarily. Everyone deserves some downtime. Modern life is stressful and hectic and so we need times when we let go of our responsibilities and just do something fun. We can still draw benefits from hobbies that are not generally considered constructive – for example, we can develop our abilities to work in teams by doing team sports, and we can increase our attention spans by reading a novel with long chapters!
Examiner:	Do people have more free time now than in the past?
Candidate:	It's a strange irony that although we now have so many labour-saving devices such as washing machines and dishwashers, we feel we have less free time. Many of my acquaintances are always complaining that they are too busy. But actually I think our ancestors had less free time than us. The average worker hardly ever got any time off and worked six or seven days a week.

Tracks 05–09

See pages 62–63 for text.

Track 10

I'm afraid I don't know what 'recreation' means.

Track 11

1   When I hear music from the 70s, it really takes me back. It makes me feel like I'm a teenager again, the memories are so vivid. So many things from that period of my life left a lasting impression on me, like meeting my first girlfriend and sitting my A levels in sweltering heat. It's still fresh in my mind.

2   I can barely remember what I did yesterday let alone events from my childhood. Well, having said that, I have some vague memories. I remember a teacher I really liked called ... Oh, the name escapes me. But she was so brilliant at explaining things and was really kind when my brother was taken ill. Oh what was her name? It's on the tip of my tongue! Anyway, as I said, I have a bad memory.

3   I often reminisce about the good old days. You have to be careful though because it's easy to get sentimental and see everything through rose-tinted glasses. Things weren't perfect back then but you often only remember the good times. I love looking at old photos. They remind me of people I'd long forgotten about and then it all comes flooding back, like my old friend Alice who passed away ten years ago. Can it really be that long? Doesn't time fly!

Track 12

1   Most children I know are well brought up.
2   I had a strict upbringing.
3   Good parenting is all about teaching a child to have good manners.
4   When I was young, I respected my elders.
4   When I was a child, my dad told me off more often than my mum.
6   I always did as I was told.
7   Children in my country generally help around the house.

Track 13

What is your most vivid childhood memory?
Are you still in touch with your childhood friends?

What was your favourite toy when you were a child?
Is it important for children to have fun? Why?

Sample answers:

Examiner: What is your most vivid childhood memory?

Candidate: Without a doubt it's getting my two pet tortoises for my sixth birthday. It was such a surprise and I was so pleased because none of my friends had such unusual pets. They were tiny – they could both sit in the palm of my hand – and I really enjoyed looking after them.

Examiner: Are you still in touch with your childhood friends?

Candidate: Some of them, yes. We've all moved on and have very different lives now, but it's nice to catch up from time to time and reminisce. You may have more in common with more recent friends but childhood friends feel almost like brothers and sisters, and there's something very special about that relationship.

Examiner: What was your favourite toy when you were a child?

Candidate: I always liked toys other children had! For example, a toy-car garage with various levels and ramps. That was great fun. My best friend had it and whenever I went over to his house I would ask to play with it. Sometimes he didn't want to, so I played with it on my own. I loved making the cars whizz around the tracks and crash into each other!

Examiner: Is it important for children to have fun?

Candidate: It is important because I believe children learn a lot through play. They learn about the world around them, they learn how to interact with other people, they learn about possible dangers through acting them out. Children shouldn't be made to grow up too fast, they should be allowed to experience the world of make-believe first. They spend long enough in the real world as adults.

Track 14

Sample answers:

Candidate: I grew up very far from most of my family so I only saw them once a year. Every summer I would go to stay with them, while my parents continued working. Although I missed my parents, I used to really enjoy spending time with my grandparents, cousins, aunts and uncles. I spent all summer there, nearly two whole months, so from time to time my cousins and I would get bored. We would ask my grandparents if they had any ideas for interesting things we could do. Sometimes they suggested going for a bike ride, sometimes into town to do some shopping. At other times, they showed us a new game to play. Then we were happy again.

One day – it must be about 25 years ago (doesn't time fly!) – all of us got really, really bored and we kept complaining to my grandparents. They were tearing their hair out, trying to think up ideas of where we could go and what we could do. Suddenly, my granddad came up with the idea of going to a new water park that had opened that summer. I hadn't heard about it but my cousins had, and they told me all about it. It was a park with vast numbers of different pools, some inside, some outside. There were water slides as well. And, on top of that, there was not one, but two playgrounds with swings, a merry-go-round, see-saws. We were so excited.

We set off and on the way we were all singing songs and laughing. We couldn't wait to get there. When we arrived, my cousins and I ran into the park and changed into our swimming costumes. Then we went looking for the most exciting-looking pool, and we found it, one with brightly coloured tiles and slides, we jumped straight in. We played all day in the park and had a lovely lunch, sat on some benches in the sunshine.

My granddad loved a pool that was filled with spa water. It was dark brown and stank of rotten eggs. I didn't want to go in but he eventually convinced me. I'm pleased he did because the water was really warm. I'd never swam in water that warm. I didn't want to get out, despite the terrible smell.

I consider it such a happy memory because we enjoyed ourselves so much and I remember so vividly how I felt that day. But there's more to it than just that. When I look back now, I understand how caring my grandparents were and how much they wanted us all to be happy. They would have done anything to help us have a good time. I appreciate that more now that I'm older and have children of my own. I hope we thanked them; I can't remember. But, anyway, they were content, I'm sure, to just watch us have an amazing time, playing and laughing in the water. So, as you can see, it was a wonderful day and is one of my favourite childhood memories.

Examiner: What other activity did you use to enjoy when you were staying with your family?

Candidate: I loved going for walks in the local park. There were people selling all kinds of delicious foods from carts, so my grandparents would invariably buy us some treat, like homemade ice-cream or cakes.

Tracks 15–18

See pages 66–68 for text.

Track 19

Childhood

Do you think people often idealise their childhoods?
How does a person's childhood influence what kind of adult they become?
When does a child become an adult in your view?

Upbringing

Do you agree with the saying 'children should be seen and not heard'?
Is it good for children to be exposed to frightening and sad experiences or should they be protected from these as far as possible?
Are children in your country generally well brought up?

Sample answers:

Examiner: Do you think people often idealise their childhoods?

Candidate: Certainly they do. The older we get, the more nostalgic we get about the past. It's only normal. And why should we dwell on the negatives? I don't think it does any harm to idealise a bit if it makes us happy to remember things in a more positive light. The only danger is that it may make us unhappy with our current lots to believe that everything was so much better back then.

Examiner: How does a person's childhood influence what kind of adult they become?

Candidate: Well, I suppose the adult you become is influenced by three main factors: firstly, your childhood, that is 'nurture'; then, your genes, that is 'nature'; and last but not least, the choices you make as an adult. To my mind, of all three, nurture has the greatest impact. They've conducted research on twins who were separated at birth and, while there are undoubtedly many similarities between them, they are also very different in many key ways: their success in the world of work, their relationships with other people. I think all this is influenced by the role models we have throughout our childhoods.

Examiner:	When does a child become an adult in your view?
Candidate:	That's a difficult question to answer and all societies grapple with this issue. It is, of course, critical for the criminal justice system to define an 'adult' correctly, or at least try to, because if somebody commits a crime as a child, they get treated more leniently than if they commit a crime as an adult. So I suppose you have to decide when you think people become fully responsible for their actions. I wouldn't want to be the one making that decision. I just don't know.
Examiner:	Do you agree with the saying 'children should be seen and not heard'?
Candidate:	I'm assuming this means that children should respect their elders and not create havoc by being noisy and answering adults back. I have some sympathy with this view. However, moderation is usually the best course to take in all things, as with upbringing. Children should respect their elders, which involves doing as they're told. Too many children nowadays think they run the household, making demands, etc. However, it is also true that a child is part of the family, too and also deserves respect. I think this means they should be allowed to express their points of view and they should be listened to and consulted. It's a fine balance, I suppose.
Examiner:	Is it good for children to be exposed to frightening and sad experiences or should they be protected from these as far as possible?
Candidate:	I don't think they should experience too many sad or terrifying experiences, if it can be helped. Nevertheless, what is very useful for teaching children about these darker sides of life without scarring them is stories. In stories they can learn about evil and the dangers in the world around them, but in a controlled way where the 'baddies' are punished and everyone ends up happy. This gives them a focus for the fears that all children have but it is a fictional one so doesn't upset their peace of mind.
Examiner:	Are children in your country generally well brought up?
	My instinct is to say 'no' because you see many misbehaving children when you're out and about. In reality, there are probably many more well brought up children than badly brought up ones, it's just that the good children don't attract your attention as much.

Track 20

1 Back in the 1960s, this was a nice place to live. Everyone knew everyone and people looked out for each other. I'm sorry to say that, since the 60s, the population has risen dramatically and this has led to a breakdown in the community ties that used to unite us. Also, second-home owners buy holiday homes here, and that has meant that the price of property has escalated in recent years, forcing young people to move away from the area.

2 My city is becoming more and more vibrant as time goes on. I love it! It used to be really dull, with nothing much for young people to do, but now bars and clubs have begun opening up. The city's no longer just for the older generations, with theatres and museums – it's got a new lease of life, with a great nightlife and an increasing student population to enjoy it.

3 A century ago, this town was a hive of activity, with its many factories and its port. Nowadays, however, it's nowhere near as bustling, as manufacturing has moved elsewhere. But I, for one, don't bewail the changes. There's a certain poignancy and beauty to the disused industrial architecture. And, in fact, many of the old factories are being converted into flats, and they're extremely popular with trendy young couples who are now moving into the town.

Track 21

Tell me about your hometown.
In what ways has your town or city changed since you were a child?

How could your town or city be improved?
Are there any traffic problems where you live?

Sample answers:

Examiner: Tell me about your hometown.

Candidate: It's a biggish town in the south of the country, with a population of about 150,000. When I was growing up, I always thought my hometown was all right but now that I've travelled more widely, I know I wouldn't want to live there anymore.

Examiner: In what ways has your town or city changed since you were a child?

Candidate: Well, crime has been on the increase since the early 90s. My friends who still live there no longer feel that safe. Also, it has become very congested and traffic is a real problem. When I visit it now, it makes me quite sad thinking how things used to be.

Examiner: How could your town or city be improved?

Candidate: The city where I live now is beautiful and it's hard for me to think of any way in which it could be improved. I suppose if I had to find something, I'd say that it has mainly chain restaurants and shops, so we could do with a greater range of independent places. It would make eating out and shopping more enjoyable.

Examiner: Are there any traffic problems where you live?

Candidate: Yes, but I think there are traffic problems everywhere in this country, certainly in all the towns and cities. Here, public transport is really expensive, so everyone drives and that means we have standstill traffic during the rush hour. They should increase the affordability of the buses.

Track 22

Sample answers:

Candidate: A place that I enjoy visiting is Graz. It's the second-largest city in Austria, with a population of around 300,000. It lies in the south-east of the country, in the state of Styria, which is a green, lush part of Austria.

There is lots to do in Graz. It has several universities, so first and foremost it's a fantastic place to be a student. It's buzzing, with a good nightlife, good restaurants and a lively cultural life. In fact, it's a UNESCO World Heritage Site and Europe's capital of culture a few years back.

If you climb up to the hill overlooking the old town, you have an amazing view of the city. What strikes me most when I go up there is all the traditional, pale buildings with their red roofs, and then right in the middle of it all, a remarkable piece of contemporary architecture, the museum of modern art. It looks like a huge sea cucumber, completely out of keeping with all the architecture around it, but of course totally *in* keeping with what it houses – modern art. I always think how brave it was of the Austrians to put it there, in the heart of the city, and how unlikely it was that that sort of thing would ever be allowed where I live! I really admire them for it and I think the building has its own kind of beauty.

The last time I went to Graz, they were having a wine festival. People were tasting all kinds of wines from stalls on the street, very informally and chatting with friends while they drank. It was wonderful.

How has it changed since I first visited it? Well, I would say it has undoubtedly become more trendy. Like I say, they have built a stunning new museum. They have also built an island in the river, which is actually a floating platform holding a café and a playground. To go with the sea-cucumber theme, this one is shaped like a sea shell. I would say the local inhabitants have become more overtly proud of their city, too. It has received quite a bit of recognition in recent times, which has really placed Graz well and truly on the cultural map; something the inhabitants are always happy to talk to you about. In fact, that is something else I enjoy about going there: the local people are invariably friendly and helpful.

Examiner: When did you last go to Graz?

Candidate: I last went there the year before last. I wish I could go more often, but unfortunately work commitments mean I can't.

Tracks 23–24

See page 76 for text.

Track 25

Home

Is it only children who experience homesickness?
Do you think it's better for children to grow up in the city or the country?
Why do some people retire to the countryside?

Patriotism

Are people from your country patriotic?
Why do people often feel proud of where they come from?
Does intense patriotism have any disadvantages?

Sample answers:

Examiner: Is it only children who experience homesickness?

Candidate: Children probably feel homesickness more acutely because they may never have been away from home before, and because they are still closely attached to their parents. They cannot appreciate the cultural insights of a new place, or the time off work, the way an adult can. And they are generally less flexible when it comes to coping with unfamiliar food and so on. However, many adults also experience culture shock when they visit a new place, which I suppose can be considered a kind of 'adult homesickness'. We find a place strange and even slightly disturbing, and this is because it is different to what we are used to. So, in a sense, we miss our familiar surroundings and are indeed homesick.

Examiner: Do you think it's better for children to grow up in the city or the country?

Candidate: I think the perfect solution is to live in the countryside close to a major cultural centre, by which I mean a big city. This means that the child can enjoy all the pleasures of country life – the farm animals, the fresh air, the relative safety – whilst at the same time not being too far from all the fun that can be had in the city – musicals, kids' museums, zoos. Kids need to be exposed to a wide range of situations and settings, and experiencing just the city or just the countryside is limiting.

Examiner: Why do some people retire to the countryside?

Candidate: I suppose they crave the peace and quiet after a lifetime of hard work in the hustle and bustle of the city. In fact, in the modern imagination, I think the city is associated with work and the country with relaxation. Of course, people like farmers do work in the countryside, so it's not an altogether accurate picture, but nevertheless it is how the two opposing settings are often regarded.

Examiner:	Are people from your country patriotic?
Candidate:	On the whole, I would say yes they are. I think most people in the world are patriotic. You can see this at the Olympics where thousands of people go to support their countries' sportspeople and millions if not billions more watch from the comfort of their own homes, cheering their countrymen on and willing them to win. It's a very powerful force, patriotism, and has been responsible for much good and bad. But I think the Olympics shows us the best and most inclusive side of patriotism.
Examiner:	Why do people often feel proud of where they come from?
Candidate:	People feel the need to belong, to a club, to a family, to a group of friends, to a region, and to a country. Where you come from is tied up with so many other things that it says an awful lot about you, and so is of the utmost importance in defining who you are. For example, it affects what you eat, what language you speak, and how you behave towards others. Being proud of where you are from is therefore an extension of being proud of who you are.
Examiner:	Does intense patriotism have any disadvantages?
Candidate:	Oh, undoubtedly. The flipside of patriotism is xenophobia, people disliking others who are from another country and associating all kinds of negative characteristics with them. People are capable of believing that everyone from 'that country over there' is mean, rude, dirty et cetera. It's quite frightening, really, because it could be argued that xenophobia has made it easier for governments to justify going to war with other nations over the centuries.

Tracks 26–29

See page 79 for text.

Track 30

What is the most important festival in your country?
Do you think this festival will still be as important in the future?
Tell me how weddings are celebrated in your country.
What are some forms of traditional dancing in your country?

Sample answers:

Examiner:	What is the most important festival in your country?
Candidate:	Our most important festival is without doubt Christmas. We all look forward to it for months, buying presents for our loved ones and decorating our homes. It's magical for everyone but for children especially. When we knew Father Christmas was about to visit, my sister Samantha and I were always too excited to sleep.
Examiner:	Do you think this festival will still be as important in the future?
Candidate:	Yes, I think so. I think people often forget the true meaning of Christmas, though – I mean, they don't think about the story of the birth of Jesus – and in the future they'll probably remember it even less. They see it more as a time for buying and receiving presents.
Examiner:	Tell me how weddings are celebrated in your country.
Candidate:	Well, the wedding party is the most interesting bit. After the ceremony, everyone has a huge meal and then dances all night, sometimes to traditional music played by a band, sometimes just to pop music played by a DJ. I prefer the traditional music because you can hear pop music any time, and the old, traditional songs have so much meaning and history behind them. The older generation always know all the words so they sing along!
Examiner:	What are some forms of traditional dancing in your country?
Candidate:	Folk dancing is quite popular, even among young people. The dancers wear traditional costume, which looks beautiful. My favourite is a circle dance performed by women, but there's also a marching dance and a couple dance. I'm afraid I don't know anything about the choreography of these dances. I just know I like watching them.

Tracks 31 & 32

Our most important festival is without doubt Christmas. We all look forward to it for months, buying presents for our loved ones and decorating our homes. It's magical for everyone but for children especially. When we knew Father Christmas was about to visit, my sister Samantha and I were always too excited to sleep.

Tracks 33–36

See pages 82–83 for text.

Track 37

Sample answers:

Candidate: I love Guy Fawkes Night. It's a British celebration held on 5th November every year. The origins of it are really fascinating, a story of intrigue and deception. In 1605, Guy Fawkes planted some gunpowder under the Houses of Parliament. He wanted to blow up the government and the King, but he was caught. He was tortured and executed for treason.

People lit bonfires to celebrate the fact that King James had survived, and the government made the day a national day of thanksgiving. People still light bonfires to this day, and for this reason, the festival is sometimes called Bonfire Night. A cloth 'Guy' is put on top of the bonfire and burned. People also set off fireworks in their back gardens or they attend public firework displays.

When I was younger, my dad would set off fireworks in our garden and I would be terrified. They were so loud they made me jump! But I had to try and hide it because he had gone to a lot of trouble to prepare and light the fireworks for us. Our cat hated Bonfire Night and would hide behind the sofa for hours on end!

I love this festival for many reasons. Firstly, it brings some colour and excitement to an otherwise very dark time of year. Then, I love the story behind it. It's so much more fascinating than the stories behind other festivals. Last but not least, I love the fact that it's a major celebration that is particular to the British. I don't think the British are too good at national celebrations, probably a result of our Puritan past. But the 5th of November is a valued exception.

It also amuses me that while the French celebrate Bastille Day, the anniversary of when revolutionaries stormed the Bastille Prison representing royal authority, we celebrate Guy Fawkes Night, the anniversary of when a plan to kill the King failed and the status quo was upheld. It says quite a lot about the differences between our cultures.

Examiner: Do you think everyone in Britain knows about the origins of the festival?

Candidate: Yes, I do. There's even a rhyme to help you remember: Remember, remember the 5th of November. Gunpowder, treason and plot. I see no reason why gunpowder treason should ever be forgot.

Track 38

This year, I'm spending New Year with my boyfriend's family. We're arriving on 28th December and staying till 4th January. I'm really looking forward to it.

Tracks 39–43

See pages 84–86 for text.

Track 44

Historical sites

Are historical sites in your country popular with visitors?
Is it more important to preserve historical sites or make way for the developments of the future?
What do you think will happen to your country's historical sites in the future?

Culture – past, present and future

What is 'culture' for you?
Do you think that it is important for a society or culture to have a sense of continuity with the past?
How will your country's culture have changed in fifty years' time?

Sample answers:

Examiner: Are historical sites in your country popular with visitors?

Candidate: They seem to be very popular, yes. The last time I went to visit a historical site myself, I was struck by the number of families there with young children. I don't think these sites are popular with young couples, necessarily, but it looks to me as though when those couples have children they suddenly develop a new appreciation for those places and I suppose they think that finding out about the history of their region and country is an important component in bringing up their children.

Examiner: Is it more important to preserve historical sites or make way for the developments of the future?

Candidate: When a developer wants to build a new shopping centre in my country, for example, they are obliged to conduct an archeological survey. If any remains are found, archeologists have to be given time to study it. I think this is marvellous. So I think old and new can work side by side and you don't necessarily have to choose between them.

Examiner: What do you think will happen to your country's historical sites in the future?

Candidate: I think many of them will continue to be given funding because people realise that you can make lots of money by attracting visitors to historical sites. On the other hand, some are so dilapidated that they require enormous amounts of investment and I'm not sure they will survive into the future – some old manor houses, for example.

Examiner: What is 'culture' for you?

Candidate: Culture can be defined as the way of life of a particular society or section of society. It involves their customs and traditions, and so in some senses culture is what distinguishes us from others, what makes us unique. I think culture is also what connects us to our past, to our heritage. We mustn't forget modern culture either, though. Youth culture is often very vibrant and powerful, with its new and inventive forms of music, dress and art.

Examiner: Do you think that it is important for a society or culture to have a sense of continuity with the past?

Candidate: Yes, definitely. Change is necessary, but it is also frightening. For this reason, people continue to rely on their traditions to give them a sense of their roots and to remind them of where they've come from. Commemorating the past is also a way of bringing people together, such as during Independence Day.

Examiner: How will your country's culture have changed in fifty years' time?

Candidate: We are becoming more and more multicultural, so I'm not sure that all of our traditions will survive in their current form. For example, can we continue to regard Christmas as our major annual celebration if perhaps half of the country does not have Christianity as its religion? It would be a shame to lose our traditions. However, if that is indeed the case, something new will I'm sure have replaced them in fifty years' time. And maybe it is better to develop new customs and celebrations that more accurately reflect modern society.

Track 45

1 Would you feel nervous about going on holiday alone?
2 Do you enjoy travelling with your family?
3 Are you scared of flying?
4 Have you been away this year?
5 Do you like to try and learn the language of the country you're travelling to?
6 Are there any differences between what young people like to do on holiday and what older people like to do?
7 Did you have a good time on your last holiday?
8 Do you mind roughing it?
9 If you won £1,000,000, would you spend it on a round-the-world trip?

Track 46

Is your country popular with tourists?
What sights and activities would you recommend to a tourist visiting your town or region?
Do you enjoy active holidays?
Tell me what your ideal holiday would be.

Sample answers:

Examiner: Is your country popular with tourists?

Candidate: Oh yes, it is. It's a key tourist destination. It isn't popular with sunseekers because, well, we don't get a lot of sun, but people who are into culture and history love it. We get millions of visitors every year.

Examiner: What sights and activities would you recommend to a tourist visiting your town or region?

Candidate: There are a great number of ancient sites near here, for example burial mounds and stone circles. They're fascinating and I wouldn't hesitate to recommend them to anyone. Luckily, it's actually better if the weather is misty or dismal when you're visiting those sites because it just adds to the atmosphere!

Examiner: Do you enjoy active holidays?

Candidate: Yes, I certainly do. I hate just sitting on a beach. I love hiking. Last year I went hiking in Nepal with some friends. It was incredibly tough but really rewarding and I got very fit and trim. We want to do something similar next year if we can save enough money.

Examiner: Tell me what your ideal holiday would be.

Candidate: My ideal holidays are when I discover new things, so I wouldn't say I have one ideal holiday in mind. But it's true that I would love to go to South America, especially Peru. I believe it's great for hikers and the landscape just looks breathtaking. I speak some Spanish too so I could communicate with the locals.

Track 47

Sample answers:

Candidate: I'd like to tell you about the time I went backpacking around Spain. I can't quite believe it but it was over a decade ago now. Two friends and I got very good-value rail passes and travelled around Spain for three months. It was an unforgettable experience.

We started off in Madrid because that's where we landed. We did some sightseeing – we especially loved the parks – and we ate and drank lots – our favourite thing was, of course, the delicious ham. We liked the nightlife in Madrid, too, not least eating out – it was a real experience. The locals don't go out to dinner until really late, often as late as 11pm (I suppose because it's so hot)! So if you turn up at a restaurant at what would be a normal time where we come from, the place is either closed or completely empty.

We then journeyed on to Santiago de Compostela in the north-west, which was fabulous, and my friend is really into art so we had to visit the Guggenheim Museum in Bilbao in the north. The weather was dreadful while we were there so we didn't get the best impression, but even so we enjoyed it. More people should visit that part of Spain.

Then we moved on to Barcelona, Madrid's rival city. We fell in love with it. It's so different to Madrid, more Bohemian in feel and more multi-cultural. The Gaudí architecture is so wonderfully whacky, looking half the time like it's fallen off the page of a fairy tale. We were quite sorry to leave Barcelona.

After that we saw Valencia, but not for long unfortunately, and then we went on to Granada. What a beautiful, beautiful place. There is nothing quite like the Moorish palace, the Alhambra, lit up at night. The image has stayed with me.

We had wanted to visit Seville and the Extremadura region of the country, but we'd run out of money by then so sadly we had to leave.

It was a memorable holiday because I was with two good friends experiencing all these amazing cities. I don't think I could do it now, because travelling so much in a relatively short time is tiring, but we were young and carefree and so took it in our stride. It was the holiday of a lifetime.

Examiner: Why did you choose to go to Spain?

Candidate: Well, one of my friends spoke Spanish really well so it seemed the obvious choice. I don't like going to a country without speaking any of the language. And my friend taught us both Spanish as we travelled round the country so by the end we could order our food ourselves and talk to people, albeit not on any complex subjects.

Track 48

See page 92 for text.

Track 49

1   I gather you're from New Zealand.
2   Saudi Arabia has an extremely cold climate.
3   Is the capital of England Tokyo?
4   Scotland lies to the south of England.

Track 50

See page 93 for text.

Track 51

a   Although it's more expensive, many people **do** go abroad for their holidays.
b   We nearly decided not to go to South Africa, but in the end we **did** go.
c   I **do** love being able to lie in when I'm on holiday.

Track 52

The benefits of travel

Do you think it's true that travel broadens the mind?

Do young people and older people benefit differently from travelling?
How can you make sure you get the most from your travels?

The impact of tourism

What are the positive impacts of tourism?
What about the negative impacts of tourism?
How has tourism impacted tourist sites in your country?

Sample answers:

Examiner: Do you think it's true that travel broadens the mind?

Candidate: I do, yes. I wouldn't want to disparage people who haven't travelled because that is almost invariably due to a lack of opportunity. I doubt any of my great-grandparents' generation ever travelled anywhere. But I can't help but think that it does make you a more open-minded person, as you see different ways of living, eating, drinking, interacting with others, and it allows you to see your own culture more objectively. It also leads to you having a wider range of experiences and makes you more interesting to talk to.

Examiner: Do young people and older people benefit differently from travelling?

Candidate: I think younger people tend to enjoy adventure and having fun. And older people value relaxation more because they have so many responsibilities at home that what they want more than anything is to 'switch off' when they go away. Of course, that's a generalisation and only takes you so far. I know it's true of me, though.

Examiner: How can you make sure you get the most from your travels?

Candidate: I've always thought learning something of the language of the country you're going to is the best possible way of benefitting fully from your holiday. That way, the local population aren't so likely to see you as an outsider, but rather as someone who has made the effort of learning some words and expressions, and so has an interest in their culture.

Examiner: What are the positive impacts of tourism?

Candidate: They are manifold. Tourism brings investment and better infrastructure to poorer communities. This means that tourists find it easier to get around, but it also leads to an improved quality of life for the local people. It also brings about greater work opportunities for the local community. Previously, for example, they may just have had fishing or farming, but tourism opens up the possibility of higher earning jobs.

Examiner: What about the negative impacts of tourism?

Candidate: Well, I've seen areas where large numbers of visitors have had a detrimental effect on local habitats. For example, coral reefs in the Caribbean. It's really tragic. The best solution, as far as the wildlife is concerned, would be to ban tourism for a few decades to let the reefs recover, but, of course, the local economy has come to rely on tourism and there would be an uproar if the government were to take that drastic step.

Examiner: How has tourism impacted tourist sites in your country?

Candidate: I think, because my country is not a big tourist destination yet, the small number of visitors we get have had only a positive effect. For example, small souvenir shops now have a larger clientele because of the visitors coming to see our temples.

Track 53

Hello. My name is Pauline Jenkins. Could you tell me your full name, please?
Thank you. Can you show me your identification, please?... All right. That's fine. I'd now like to ask you some questions about yourself. Tell me about where you live.
What are the advantages of living there?
What are the disadvantages of living there?

We're now going to talk about animals. What is your favourite animal?

Why do you think some people like keeping pets?

Are there any animals you are scared of?

Are zoos popular in your country?

Let's move on to talk about food. Do you think men or women make the best cooks?

Is it important to teach children to cook from a young age?

What is a typical dish from your country or region?

Do people in your country or region eat traditional food or international food?

Track 54

Now, I'm going to give you a topic and I'd like you to talk about it for one to two minutes. You'll have one minute to think about what you're going to say before you begin talking. You can make some notes if you wish. Here is a pencil and some paper. I'd like you to describe a personal achievement you are proud of.

Track 55

All right. Remember, you have one to two minutes to talk on the topic. Don't worry if I stop you. I'll let you know when the time is up. Please start speaking now.

Track 56

We've been talking about achievements. I'd like to discuss with you some more questions related to this topic. First, let's consider the role of achievements in the world of education. Do you think that in your country academic success is more valued than other kinds of achievement, such as achievements in sport?

In your opinion, is it recognition and prizes that motivate students to succeed, or is it a personal sense of achievement?

What do you think makes some students more successful than others?

Now, we're going to discuss motivation and achievement in the workplace. Some people think that a successful person is someone who earns a lot of money. Do you agree?

Would you say workers in your country were motivated primarily by money?

Do you think people in your country take the same pride in their work as they used to in the past?

Thank you. It's been nice talking to you.

Track 57

Sample answers:

Examiner:	Hello. My name is Pauline Jenkins. Could you tell me your full name, please?
Candidate:	Hello. My name is Marie Dupont.
Examiner:	Thank you. Can you show me your identification, please?... All right. That's fine. I'd now like to ask you some questions about yourself. Tell me about where you live.
Candidate:	I live in Paris, the capital city of France. It's very famous for being a romantic city, the city of love.
Examiner:	What are the advantages of living there?
Candidate:	It's lively and fun and you never get bored. You can find any kind of entertainment you can imagine, from bars and clubs to museums and galleries.
Examiner:	What are the disadvantages of living there?
Candidate:	It's very crowded, and quite dirty in parts. You have to know which areas to avoid too, as some areas have bad reputations, especially at night.

Examiner:	We're now going to talk about animals. What is your favourite animal?
Candidate:	My favourite animal is the cat. I love cats because they're a lot of fun, very playful, but also seem to have bit of character. So, it's always quite amusing to try to play with your cat.
Examiner:	Why do you think some people like keeping pets?
Candidate:	I would suspect it's mainly for the company, so that they don't feel alone when they come home in the evening and they have someone waiting for them. I don't have any pets, though I used to when I was a kid.
Examiner:	Are there any animals you are scared of?
Candidate:	I have a phobia of snakes. I reckon it's because of the way the creature looks and they can also be venomous. They're aggressive so if they bite you, you can get very badly hurt. Spiders are another animal I'm terrified of. I hate the fast, erratic way they move.
Examiner:	Are zoos popular in your country?
Candidate:	Yes, they are, especially with kids. Kids love discovering new things, including new animals, and a zoo is the best place to do that. They can observe a wide range of animals in a safe environment.
Examiner:	Let's move on to talk about food. Do you think men or women make the best cooks?
Candidate:	It doesn't depend on the sex of the person but on their enthusiasm. The men in my family are really good cooks, and they enjoy talking about food as well as cooking and eating it.
Examiner:	Is it important to teach children to cook from a young age?
Candidate:	The younger the better. Of course, you wouldn't give a young child a knife, but they can mix ingredients together and things like that. The younger they start, the better cooks they'll be when they grow up.
Examiner:	What is a typical dish from your country or region?
Candidate:	Lots of people think we eat frogs' legs all the time. It's a kind of national stereotype. But actually I've never eaten them! I would say a more typical dish is steak with chips, and it's one of my favourites.
Examiner:	Do people in your country or region eat traditional food or international food?
Candidate:	We eat both. I regard it as very important to keep culinary traditions alive, but I also love Chinese food and Japanese food and Indian food, and loads of other cuisines. I like having variety in my diet.
Examiner:	Now I'm going to give you a topic and I'd like you to talk about it for one to two minutes. You'll have one minute to think about what you're going to say before you begin talking. You can make some notes if you wish. Here is a pencil and some paper. I'd like you to describe a personal achievement you are proud of.
Examiner:	All right. Remember, you have one to two minutes to talk on the topic. Don't worry if I stop you. I'll let you know when the time is up.
Candidate:	OK.
Examiner:	Please start speaking now.
Candidate:	OK, so you asked me to talk about an achievement I'm particularly proud of, so I could have talked about when I passed my university exams, or when I bought my first home, but in the end, I decided to talk about the only time I actually won a sports tournament.
	Only once did I win my village tennis tournament. It was when I was fifteen years old. It was particularly difficult because, to be honest, I'm not a great tennis player and I always played mainly to have fun and not really to win. But that one year I decided. I made it my goal: I was going to win the village tennis tournament. So I played many matches, lots of them against older players, much older than me, who were members of the club, in their fifties, and it was very difficult. Playing older players is always tough. They have more experience, they do all these impressive tricks and they definitely know how to beat their opponent. And on top of that it's very much a matter of pride for them – they don't want to lose against one of the younger members of the club.

But anyway, I won a few matches against older players and then I ended up playing the final against my best friend. And that was another difficulty. He was my best friend so I didn't want to play it too mean with him but at the same time I wanted to win. At least the fact that he was my best friend meant that I knew exactly how to beat him, though, because I had played against him many times before. We had a very long game and it was nerve-wracking. It wasn't very good tennis but in the end I won.

I'm very proud of my achievement because I managed to reach the goal I set for myself and it was something that I know neither the spectators nor the other players would have expected me to accomplish.

Examiner: Thank you. Was your family proud that you won the tournament?

Candidate: Yes, they were. We had a big meal to celebrate, and my dad cooked all my favourite things. He's a great cook so that was a real treat for me.

Examiner: We've been talking about achievements. I'd like to discuss with you some more questions related to this topic. First, let's consider the role of achievements in the world of education. Do you think that in your country academic success is more valued than other kinds of achievement, such as achievements in sport?

Candidate: No, I don't. I think in my country, successful sportspeople are looked up to more in society at large as well as at school.

Examiner: Why do you think that is?

Candidate: Well, I think people who are good students are often thought of as nerds and are teased by their classmates, whereas being good at sport is considered 'cool'. Maybe this is due to the role of celebrity sportspeople, David Beckham being the most prominent among them in recent years. They are chased by the paparazzi, and given lucrative sponsorship deals and so on.

Examiner: Yes, I see. In your opinion, is it recognition and prizes that motivate students to succeed, or is it a personal sense of achievement?

Candidate: I would say they hanker after recognition from their teachers and perhaps envy from other students. I know that was the case with me, if I'm honest! It may be, though, that if someone is particularly timid, they would actually shy away from any special recognition of their efforts.

Examiner: Right. And what do you think makes some students more successful than others?

Candidate: Although, as I said, most students are motivated by recognition, I do think that those who are the most successful in the long run are those who have intrinsic motivation. And that is because you don't always get congratulated publicly for everything you do, so someone who does things only for that, would soon stop making an effort, you know?

Examiner: Yes, that's a good point. Now, we're going to discuss motivation and achievement in the workplace. Some people think that a successful person is someone who earns a lot of money. Do you agree?

Candidate: No, I would define it as 'someone who benefits others'?

Examiner: Right. Can you explain what you mean?

Candidate: Yes, I mean that working just for the money could be considered selfish. Most people do it, and I don't judge people for having that as their primary objective. Nevertheless, those who work to help others are more inspirational: nurses, for example, who really don't earn much, or youth workers, who often don't get much appreciation for their hard work, or those who do volunteer work with the homeless or something like that.

Examiner: Yes, so you would say that most workers in your country were motivated primarily by money?

Candidate: I would, yes. It's only normal. People have families to feed and, given the choice of a low-paid job that benefitted others and a higher-paid job that benefitted their own family, it's only reasonable that most would choose the latter. It's possible that those who choose the former kind of job are single or young, and so don't have that many responsibilities.

Examiner:	OK. And what about how things in the workplace have changed? Do you think people in your country take the same pride in their work as they used to?
Candidate:	Hmm, that's a tough question. I'm inclined to say 'no'.
Examiner:	Why do you say that?
Candidate:	Because many people in my country now work for huge companies. They may never even have seen their managing director and certainly don't know him very well. They don't have any reason to take pride in doing the job to a high standard because feedback is limited. In the past, companies were not only smaller but tended to be family run, so everyone had something invested, I mean personally speaking, in the business. They cared about the success of the business.
Examiner:	Thank you. It's been nice talking to you.
Candidate:	Thank you very much.

Answer key

1 People and relationships

Vocabulary: Character and personality

Exercise 1

ambitious: Someone who is ambitious has a strong desire to be successful, rich, or powerful.

blunt: If you are blunt, you say exactly what you think without trying to be polite.

clever: Someone who is clever is intelligent and able to understand things easily or plan things well.

creative: A creative person has the ability to invent and develop original ideas, especially in the arts.

good fun: If you say that someone is good fun, you mean that you enjoy being with them because they say and do interesting or amusing things.

hard-working: If you describe someone as hard-working, you mean that they work very hard.

impatient: If you are impatient, you are easily irritated by things.

judgemental: If you say that someone is judgemental, you are critical of them because they form opinions of people and situations very quickly, when it would be better for them to wait until they know more about the person or situation.

nosy: If you describe someone as nosy, you mean that they are interested in things which do not concern them.

open-minded: If you describe someone as open-minded, you approve of them because they are willing to listen to and consider other people's ideas and suggestions.

outgoing: Someone who is outgoing is very friendly and likes meeting and talking to people.

over-sensitive: If you are over-sensitive about something, you are too easily worried and offended when people talk about it.

reliable: People that are reliable can be trusted to work well or to behave in the way that you want them to.

self-assured: Someone who is self-assured shows confidence in what they say and do because they are sure of their own abilities.

sociable: Sociable people are friendly and enjoy talking to other people.

stingy: If you describe someone as stingy, you are criticizing them for being unwilling to spend money.

Exercise 2

Positive: ambitious, clever, creative, good fun, hard-working, open-minded, outgoing, reliable, self-assured, sociable

Negative: blunt, impatient, judgemental, nosy, over-sensitive, stingy

Vocabulary: Relationships

Exercise 4

1 b, 2 g, 3 d, 4 a, 5 c, 6 h, 7 f, 8 e

Vocabulary: Modifying

Exercise 7

1 really, 2 so, 3 a bit, 4 so, 5 very, 6 so, 7 terribly, 8 quite, 9 extremely, 10 so

Grammar: Thinking about tenses

Exercise 14

1 How long have you known this person? – present perfect
2 How did you meet? – past tenses, e.g. past simple and past continuous
3 What kind of person is he/she? – present tenses, e.g. present simple and present continuous
4 Explain why you like him/her. – present tenses

Exercise 15

1 past simple (It is a completed action in the past.)
2 'd (would) + infinitive (It is a past habit.)
3 present perfect (It refers to a period of time that began in the past and continues until the present.)

Pronunciation: Weak and strong forms

Exercise 17

1 Can I have a cup <u>of</u> tea?
2 We met <u>at</u> uni.
3 I've known him <u>for</u> ten years.
4 I'm <u>from</u> Dubai.
5 It's quarter <u>to</u> ten.

Exercise 20

1 weak,   2 strong (it comes at the end
of the sentence),   3 strong (a contrast/
correction is being expressed),   4 weak

Exam technique: What it means to 'know' a word

Exercise 1

1 mate (informal) c,   2 beau (old fashioned) b,
3 bloke (informal) e,   4 folks (informal) a,
5 kinsfolk (old fashioned) d

Exercise 2

1 *folks*: noun; *formal*: adjective
2 formality (noun); formally (adverb). Also: in_formal/
in_formality/in_formally
3 *Bloke* is used in the UK.
4 *Slim* is complimentary; *skinny* can be insulting.
5 BOYfriend; aCQUAINtance
7 Other collocations with *friend* include: *a long-lost
friend, a mutual friend, an imaginary friend, be just
good friends* (not have a romantic relationship)

Exercise 3

Suggested answers:

1 in-laws /ɪnlɔːz/ Your in-laws are the parents and
close relatives of your husband or wife
2 other half /ʌðə hɑːf/ your other half is your
husband or wife
3 sibling /sɪblɪŋ/ Your siblings are your brothers and
sisters.

2   A healthy body

Vocabulary: Sports and fitness

Exercise 3

**Suggested answers could include
three from the following:**

Contact sports: boxing, judo, rugby,
taekwondo, wrestling
Water sports: diving, jet-skiing, kayaking, kite-
surfing, rowing, sailing, scuba-diving, snorkelling,
swimming, water polo, waterskiing, windsurfing
Extreme sports: abseiling, bungee jumping,
gliding, hang-gliding, rock climbing, sky diving,
snowboarding, snowmobiling, white-water rafting
Team sports: baseball, basketball, cricket,
football, field hockey, ice hockey, lacrosse,
rowing, sailing, volleyball, water polo
Individual sports: abseiling, archery, athletics,
badminton, boxing, bungee jumping, chess,

cycling, diving, fencing, figure skating, gliding,
golf, gymnastics, hang-gliding, jet-skiing,
judo, kayaking, kite-surfing, motorbike racing,
off-road, rally, rock climbing, rowing, sailing,
scuba-diving, shooting, skateboarding, skiing,
sky diving, snooker, snorkelling, snowboarding,
snowmobiling, surfing, swimming, table tennis,
taekwondo, tennis, water polo, waterskiing,
white-water rafting, windsurfing, wrestling
Note: Some sports can belong to more than one category.

Exercise 5

1   football;
2a   builds up
2b   fans;
2c   draw (drew, drawn);
2d   stadium, pitch;
2e   scored the winning goal;
2f   an up-and-coming talent;
3   lose; play away; support (a team); the latest kit;
the club; coach a junior team; train; player; a
(beautiful) header

Vocabulary: Health and diet

Exercise 7

1   Definition b
2   Definition b
3   Definition a

Exercise 8

1 malnourished;   2 metabolism;   3 carbohydrates;
4 vitamins;   5 calories;   6 a crash diet;   7 put on
weight;   8 lose weight;   9 obese;   10 underweight

Exercise 9

1 a crash diet, malnourished;   2 carbohydrates;
3 calories, obese;   4 metabolism, put on weight;
5 underweight, lose weight;   6 vitamins

Pronunciation: Expressing enthusiasm

Exercise 12

1 Speaker 1 sounds enthusiastic;   Speaker 2 sounds
bored;   Speaker 3 sounds bored; Speaker 4 sounds
enthusiastic.
2 The way people say the words tells you how they are
feeling:
Speakers 2 and 3 sound bored because
their intonation is low and falling.
Speakers 1 and 4 sound enthusiastic
because their intonation rises and then
falls dramatically.
3 The reason is usually sarcasm: we sometimes say
something that is the opposite of what we think, but

reveal what we really think with our intonation (low and falling, in these examples). We may do this to be funny and to emphasise our true feelings. Speaker 2, for example, may be a woman whose boyfriend wants to watch the match whereas she is not interested in it.

English has a particularly wide pitch range (the voice goes up and down a lot). If we are expressing strong emotions such as excitement or surprise the pitch moves up and down dramatically.

Expressing opinions

Exercise 19
Sample answers:
1 My answer may surprise you but, in my view, the most interesting sport is figure skating. I'm always on the edge of my seat, willing the skater not to fall. It's so nail-biting.
2 If you ask me, the best sport for keeping fit is without doubt swimming. It is well known that swimming uses all the major muscle groups. Not only that, it's cardiovascular exercise, which strengthens the heart and lungs.
3 I would argue that the most dangerous sport is sky diving, for obvious reasons. I know someone whose parachute failed to open properly, and she considered herself extremely lucky to just break both her legs.
4 I would say the most dangerous sports are those involving fast and powerful vehicles, like motor racing. There are very often crashes, resulting in not only injuries but on occasion fatalities too.

Exercise 20–21
Sample answers:
1 As far as I'm concerned, taxing unfit people for their health care is just ridiculous. What next? Taxing clumsy people more because they're more likely to trip and injure themselves?
2 I'm strongly in favour of making all children do at least one hour of sport a day. Obesity among children is a big problem in my country, and this initiative would help combat that.
3 I believe that imposing an additional tax on smokers is a sensible idea. After all, they do put a much bigger strain on the health system than non-smokers.
4 I must admit, I think a campaign promoting a balanced diet is another example of the government acting like a nanny state. I'm sure most people would prefer not to be patronised like that.
5 I'm not convinced raising the minimum age for alcohol consumption would work because young people would still find ways of laying their hands on alcohol, even if it's illegal.

Vocabulary: Collocations

Exercise 23
1 c/d; 2 b; 3 h; 4 d/c; 5 j; 6 a; 7 i; 8 e; 9 f; 10 g

Exercise 24
verb + adjective: keep fit, keep active
verb + noun: play volleyball
verb + adjective + noun: set a good example, lead healthy lives
noun + noun: form of exercise, sense of achievement,
adjective + noun: balanced diet, passive smoking, public places

Exam technique: Planning your answer

Exercise 1
a He will use past tenses (e.g. past simple, past continuous, past perfect) because the question asks about a completed action in the past.
b He is probably aware that he tends to speak with low, flat intonation, which can make him sound uninterested. He is reminding himself to speak with more variation in pitch so that he conveys the excitement of the match to the examiner.
c No, he is only going to reveal who won towards the end, probably to create some suspense and make his talk more interesting.
d He wants to remember to use it; using it will show he has a good vocabulary and therefore improve his mark. He has included collocations and whole phrases, not just single words.

3   Studies & work

Vocabulary: Studies and work

Exercise 3
1 art subjects, 2 qualifications, 3 tuition fees,
4 lectures, 5 seminars, 6 I failed,
7 retake, 8 passed, 9 coursework,
10 my dream job, 11 job security

Exercise 4
1 i, 2 g, 3 b, 4 c, 5 a, 6 d, 7 f, 8 h, 9 e
10 o, 11 s, 12 m, 13 l, 14 q, 15 j, 16 r
17 n, 18 p, 19 k

Exercise 5
1 unemployment; 2 presentation;
3 promotion; 4 appraisals/an appraisal;

5 laid off; 6 problematic; 7 responsibilities;
8 stressful; 9 dealing; 10 inexperienced;

Grammar: Speculating

Exercise 8

it's very likely I would need ...; I don't think
that would be a problem ...; I imagine the job
would involve ...; I suspect it would be ...

Exercise 9
Suggested answers:

It is extremely unlikely that I would be considered
clever enough to be a university lecturer!

Being a chef must be incredibly stressful.

Being a musician is, I suspect, a job that requires an
enormous amount of hard work and dedication.

I imagine that being an astronaut must be absolutely
fascinating.

It is very likely that a soldier takes great satisfaction
from serving his country.

Office juniors can't earn that much.

Exercise 10

1 The use of the first conditional with *will* suggests
that the speaker thinks getting his/her dream job is
likely.
2 The second conditional indicates that the speaker
thinks it improbable that he/she will get his/her
dream job.
3 The third conditional is used to imagine the result
of something that did not happen in the past.
Therefore, this person did not study harder and so
did not get his/her dream job.

Exercise 11

1 I'll get into university provided that I get straight
As. / Provided that I get straight As, I'll get into
university.
2 Unless my CV stands out, I will never be called for
an interview. / I will never be called for an interview
unless my CV stands out.
3 As long as I pass my final exams, I've got a chance
of getting my dream job. / I've got a chance of
getting my dream job as long as I pass my final
exams.
4 I will never be an athlete no matter how hard I train. /
No matter how hard I train, I will never be an athlete.

Pronunciation: Word stress

Exercise 14

1 leader, 2 hotel, 3 production, 4 desert

Exercise 15

1 *leader*; other examples: *earnings, payment, boring*
2 *hotel*; other examples: *balloon, insist*
3 *desert*; other examples: *conduct, contrast, progress*
4 *production*; other examples: *corruption, distraction,
recognition*

Exercise 16

1 presented: verb
2 object: verb
3 suspect: verb
4 increase: noun
5 progress: verb
6 transfer: noun
7 export: adjective

Exercise 17

O o o: interesting, motivate, seminar,
foreigner, lecturer, difficult
o O o: prestigious, frustrating, redundant, consider
o O o o: responsible, experience, security
o o O o: fundamental, entertaining, workaholic

Exam technique: Giving answers that are the right length

Exercise 1

1a This answer is too short. The candidate could also
say what kind of company he/she works for and
what his/her job is.
1b This is a good answer.
1c This answer is too long (it is closer to a Part 2 answer)
and not everything is relevant to the question; for
example, the section about becoming a doctor.
2a This answer is too abrupt and almost sounds rude.
It would, however, be acceptable to begin like this
and then give more details; for example, *I didn't
choose it. My family have an export business – we
export coffee – so I don't really have a choice, I have
to work for our family business.*
2b This is a good answer.
3a Although this answer begins with *I'm not sure.
Er ...* it is a good answer. Saying something like
I'm not sure is not a problem as long as you do not
hesitate for too long, and give a full answer without
further prompting from the examiner. In fact, using
phrases like this can be a good idea because they
give you time to think.
3b The examiner would probably not consider this a
relevant answer and may think the candidate has not
understood the question. The question asked what
was difficult about the job but this candidate is telling
the examiner what he/she does not like about the job.

4   The world around us

Vocabulary: The environment

Exercise 1
1 c; 2 f; 3 d; 4 e; 5 a; 6 g; 7 b

Vocabulary: Climate

Exercise 3
Speaker 1: Saudi Arabia;
Speaker 2: Wales;   Speaker 3: Iceland

Exercise 4
Hot: sweltering, it can exceed 50°C
Cold: wrap up warm, it never gets above 25°C
Wet: it's constantly drizzling, lush countryside
Dry: arid, precipitation is very low

Exercise 5
1 g; 2 e; 3 c; 4 i; 5 h; 6 f; 7 j; 8 b; 9 a; 10 d

Exercise 6
1 c; 2 b; 3 c; 4 c; 5 a; 6 a; 7 a; 8 b

Grammar: Cleft sentences

Exercise 9
1 It is the monsoon season that I can't stand.
2 What I want is to go to the beach.

Exercise 10
What I like most is hot, dry weather.
It's the rain that influences my mood the most.
What I really can't stand is being cold and wet.

Exercise 11
Suggested answers:
1 I like warm weather because you can spend more of
  your time outdoors.
     The reason why I like warm weather **is** because
  you can spend more of your time outdoors.
2 I spend my summers at a lake in the north of
  country.
     The place where I spend my summers **is** at a lake
  in the north of country.
3 I dislike damp weather most of all because washing
  takes forever to dry!
     The weather that I dislike most of all **is** damp
  weather because washing takes forever to dry!

Grammar: Complex sentences

Exercise 13
1 Although snow is beautiful to look at, it makes it
  difficult to get to work. OR Snow makes it difficult to
  get work although it is beautiful to look at.
2 Since it rains so much in my country, we spend a lot
  of our time indoors. OR We spend a lot of our time
  indoors since it rains so much in my country.

Grammar: Subordinate clauses

Exercise 14
Suggested answers:
1 *Although* it was windy, I walked out to the end of the
  pier.
2 We built a huge snowman *while* the snow was
  falling.
3 *Because* I want to help to protect the environment,
  I'm going to encourage everyone I know to start
  recycling. (Note: many of us are taught not to start
  a sentence with *because*, but this is becoming more
  acceptable and is used in spoken English and even
  in literature.)
4 *Whenever* the sun shines, I make the most of it by
  going to the park.
5 *Whatever* the weather, our party will go ahead.
6 *Rather than* driving to work, I've started cycling.
7 I'll go and post the letter *as soon as* it stops raining.

Pronunciation: Long and short vowel sounds

Exercise 20
a skid; b pitch; c fool; d walk

5   Communication

Vocabulary: Languages

Exercise 1
1 mother tongue;   2 multilingual; 3 fluent;
4 get by (in);   5 am (a bit) rusty;   6 pick up;
7 a global language;   8 a minority language;
9 a foreign language;   10 a widely spoken
language;   11 a second language

Exercise 2
1 b; 2 c, e; 3 d; 4 a

Vocabulary: Keeping in touch

Exercise 3
1 have lost touch;   2 keeps in touch;
3 to get back in touch

Exercise 4
Suggested answer:
Because I've moved away from my hometown, my old school friends and I can't just go round each other's houses. We keep in touch via social networking sites and by phone. Otherwise, though, I find that rather impersonal, so when it comes to friends who live nearby, I like to meet up with them for coffee.

Vocabulary: Globalisation

Exercise 5
1 integration; 2 commonly; 3 working; 4 remarkable; 5 largely; 6 technological; 7 recognisable; 8 creates/is creating; 9 global; 10 speaking

Grammar: Making comparisons

Exercise 8
much: significantly, far
a bit: slightly, marginally

Exercise 9
1 a fewer; b more
2 **Suggested answers:**
   a The more languages you speak, the greater your earning potential.
   b The greater the spread of English and the culture of English-speaking countries, the more of a threat there is to local languages and traditions.

Expressing attitude

Exercise 11
1 undoubtedly; 2 Ideally; 3 as luck would have it; 4 All things considered/Admittedly/Arguably/Undoubtedly; 5 Admittedly/Undoubtedly; 6 arguably/undoubtedly; 7 Even more importantly/Ideally

Exercise 13
Comparative and superlative structures
it's one of the most widely-spoken languages in the world
Spanish culture is becoming more and more influential internationally
It is, for example, overtaking English as the most widely-spoken language in certain parts of the USA
Spanish vocabulary would be easier for me to acquire than Spanish grammar
I understand the grammar is one of the most difficult things about the Spanish language
Speaking Spanish would definitely make my holidays a lot easier and more enjoyable.

Attitude markers
definitely; undoubtedly; obviously; luckily

Pronunciation: Consonants

Exercise 15
si<u>xth</u>; <u>str</u>ong; <u>gl</u>im<u>psed</u>; <u>three</u>

Exam technique: Giving yourself time to think

Exercise 1
Well
um
er

Exercise 3
Actually, no they don't.
Not exactly, no.

Exercise 4
Yes, they certainly are.
Precisely.

6 Technology

Vocabulary: Technology

Exercise 1
1 A technophile is someone who loves new technology. A technophobe is someone who dislikes and is afraid of new technology.
2 The writer of the text a technophile (*we're busy upgrading our MP3 players to the latest model...*).
3 Examples of *gadgets*: smartphones (mobile phones with Internet and computing capabilities), e-book readers, night-vision binoculars, digital cameras, breadmakers (a home appliance for baking bread)
4 state-of-the-art
5 outdated
6 Artificial Intelligence
7 Possible answer: I can't say it's that important to me to upgrade my mobile every few months. But it seems to matter a lot to other people, I guess because they are dazzled by the new features of the latest model. And older models quickly begin to look outdated.

Exercise 2
1a blew up; 1b blew up
2a have broken down; 2b breaks down
3a turn up; 3b turn up
4a turn ... down; 4b Turn ... down

5a turned over; 5b turn over
6a set off; 6b set off

Exercise 3
break down: become ineffective; separate into parts
turn down: reject; reduce the volume/temperature
set off: start a journey; cause sth to operate
turn up: appear; increase the volume/temperature
blow up: (cause to) explode; enlarge (a photo)
turn over: change position; watch a different TV channel

Vocabulary: The Internet

Exercise 5
1 b; 2 c; 3 a; 4 d

Vocabulary: Phrasal verb particles

Exercise 7
1 off; 2 away; 3 down; 4 in; 5 down;
6 off; 7 on; 8 in; 9 on; 10 up; 11 out;

Exercise 8
The piece of equipment I'd like to talk about is …

Pronunciation: Sentence stress

Exercise 12
1 It's a PIECE of eQUIPment.
2 The LAtest TREND is for GREEN techNOLogy.
3 Do you KNOW the PRICE of THIS?
4 We CAN'T SPEAK ENglish FLUently. Can YOU?
The function word, *you*, in sentence 4 is stressed because it comes at the end of a sentence. It is pronounced using the strong form, /juː/.

Exercise 13
2 Function words containing a schwa:
  Sentence 1: a /ə/; of /əv/
  Sentence 2: the /ðə/; for /fə/
  Sentence 3: you /jə/; the /ðə/; of /əv/
  Sentence 4: can /kən/

Exam technique: Coherence

Exercise 1
1 c, g, e, f, b, d, a
2 b Then, surgeons can perform very delicate operations in this way.
  d Last, but not least recovery time is much quicker due again to the small incisions.
  f First of all, the surgeon can operate through tiny incisions so there is less scarring.
3 So, as you see; Possible answers: *In short; So basically; To sum up*

Exercise 3
But then again

Exercise 4
On the one hand; On the other hand

Exercise 5

Subject pronouns	I	you	he	she	it	we	they
Object pronouns	me	you	him	her	it	us	them
Possessive pronouns	mine	yours	his	hers	X	ours	theirs

Exercise 6 a his; b they, they; c theirs; d it

Exercise 7 No, it is unclear. *She* could refer to *Kate* or *her mum*. Instead, the speaker should have said *Kate really enjoyed it* or *Her mum really enjoyed it*, as appropriate.

Exercise 8 them; they

7 Hobbies

Vocabulary: Likes and dislikes

Exercise 1
a *be keen on* + *-ing* or noun (+)
b *can't stand* + *-ing* or noun (–)
c *be crazy about* + *-ing* or noun (+)
d *not mind* + *-ing* or noun (indifferent)
e *be fanatical about* + *-ing* or noun (+)
f *can take it or leave it* (indifferent)
g *… is not my kind of thing* (–)

Vocabulary: Hobbies

Exercise 3
1 **Reading:** 1 page-turner; 2 set; 3 about; 4 opening; 5 character
2 **Art:** 1 exhibition; 2 hype; 3 original; 4 representational; 5 abstract; 6 work
3 **Music:** 1 taken up; 2 concert; 3 live; 4 gigs; 5 lyrics; 6 tunes; 7 charts
4 **Film:** 1 genre; 2 rom-com (romantic comedy); 3 star-studded; 4 slow-moving; 5 predictable; 6 rave;

Language: Frequency

Exercise 4
1 every single day (using *single* adds extra emphasis)

every other day (one day yes, one day
  no, one day yes, one day no…)
every Tuesday
once a fortnight
several times a year
twice a year

Grammar: Present perfect

Exercise 7
1 've lived/'ve been living; for; 've known; since
2 ever; never; already
3 announced; made
4 've lost; 've broken
5 haven't had; didn't have; 've been; was

Exercise 10
1 1 've been playing / 've played; since
  2 've been going
  3 've known; for
  4 've read
  5 've been watching

2 1 rule 1
  2 rule 4
  3 rule 1
  4 rule 2, completed action
  5 rule 3

Pronunciation: The schwa /ə/

Exercise 14
1 AUthor   YOga
  toDAY   ENgland
  SUMMer   INternet
  coLLECtion   suPPOSE
  PERson   GARdening
  LEIsure   phoTOGraphy
  FAmous   oPINion

2 The schwas are marked in bold. Note that the /ə/
  sound appears in some diphthongs, e.g. /əʊ/ as
  in yoga, when it can be stressed, but that we are
  considering the /ə/ sound alone.

  AUth**o**r   YOg**a**
  t**o**DAY   ENgl**a**nd
  SUMM**er**   INt**er**net
  coLLECti**o**n   suPPOSE
  PER**so**n   GARd**e**ning
  LEIsure   ph**o**TOGraphy
  FAm**ous**   **o**PINi**o**n

Exam technique: Sounding polite

Exercise 1
a This is too abrupt and is not something English people
  generally say. It appears rude despite the *please*.
b This is suitable. It uses a modal verb and the
  intonation is polite.
c Although the intonation here is polite, asking
  somebody in a formal situation to repeat by saying
  What? is impolite.
d This is impolite, in terms of word choice and
  intonation.

Exercise 2
1 The first is impolite, the second polite.

Exercise 4
I'm afraid I don't know what *recreation* means.

8   Youth

Vocabulary: Remembering

Exercise 1
1 1 takes; 2 vivid; 3 lasting; 4 fresh
2 1 barely; 2 vague; 3 escapes; 4 tongue
3 1 good; 2 long; 3 flooding 4 fly

Exercise 2
1 It's on the tip of my tongue.
2 Doesn't time fly!
3 It really takes me back.
4 It's still fresh in my mind.
5 It all comes flooding back.

Vocabulary: Childhood

Exercise 3
1 g; 2 i; 3 f; 4 b; 5 e; 6 c; 7 d; 8 a; 9 h;

Exercise 4
1 d; 2 f; 3 g; 4 b; 5 c; 6 h; 7 a; 8 e

Pronunciation: Past tense -*ed* endings

Exercise 8
1 enjoyed /d/   worked /t/   acted /ɪd/

Exercise 9
/d/: loved; played; aged; cycled; seemed;
agreed; answered; breathed

/t/ laughed; thanked; wished;
helped; asked; matched

/ɪd/ accepted; decided; hated; needed; wanted; pretended

Grammar: Past tenses, *used* to and *would*

Exercise 13

1 a *used to* to describe a past habit: **used to take** me to school

   b *used to* to describe a past state: I **used to live** quite far from my school

3 a *would* to describe a past habit: he **would push** my bike home

   b The strong form of *would* is /wʊd/. The weak form is /wəd/. You can also use the contraction *'d*, e.g. **I'd** /aɪd/.

Exercise 14

1 a the past simple used to describe a past state: when I **was** little

   b the past simple to describe a past habit: my granddad **let** me cycle

   c the past simple to describe a single completed action: I **looked** back

2 a I would... ~~going~~ go with him to the local park (should be *would* + infinitive)

   b I ~~would own~~ owned/used to own a horse (can't use *would* to describe long-lasting situations or past states)

   c I ~~used to see~~ saw Sam at the cinema (must use past simple for single completed actions in the past)

Exercise 15

1 the past continuous used to give background: I **was cycling** along
main action: Suddenly I **looked** back and my granddad was nowhere to be seen.

3 a 1 were jumping; 2 were enjoying; 3 walked; 4 told

   b 1 was; 2 were walking; 3 ran; 4 was barking; 5 were; 6 tried; 7 bit

Exercise 16

1 past perfect and past simple: I **cycled** back the way I **had come**; [I] **found** him lying on the ground. He **had tripped** on some loose paving.

3 1 was playing; 2 was being (Note: You are careless = You are a careless person; You are being careless = You are careless now, but usually you are not.)
3 heard; 4 went; 5 saw; 6 had broken; 7 arrived; 8 said; 9 looked; 10 gasped; 11 realised; 12 had happened; 13 blamed; 14 had asked; 15 was

9 Home

Vocabulary: Describing places

Exercise 1
City: 1; 3; 4; 6
Country: 2; 5

Exercise 2
1 1 c; 2 a; 3 d; 4 b; 5 e; 6 g; 7 h; 8 f; 9 l; 10 i; 11 n; 12 m; 13 k; 14 j

Vocabulary: Comparing now and then

Exercise 4
1 1 Back in the 1960s; 2 since the 60s; 3 in recent years

2 1 as time goes on; 2 It used to be; 3 but now

3 1 A century ago; 2 Nowadays; 3 are being converted

2 a past simple (other past tenses can also be used to describe the past); b present simple, present perfect (changes that have taken place over time), present continuous (a change still in progress)

Vocabulary: Suffixes

Exercise 6
1 1 motherhood; 2 forgetfulness; 3 addressee; 4 treatment; 5 alcoholism; 6 craftsmanship; 7 awareness; 8 employee; 9 disappointment; 10 heroism; 11 leadership; 12 neighbourhood

2 **Sample answers: -ship**: apprenticeship, sponsorship; **-ness**: completeness, fairness; **-ee**: absentee, trainee; **-ism**: sexism, Communism; **-hood**: likelihood, livelihood

3 1 shortage; 2 employment; 3 scarcity; 4 Homesickness; 5 preference

Exercise 7
1 1 mountainous; 2 roadworthy; 3 childproof; 4 messy; 5 plentiful

2 **Sample answers: -ous**: cancerous, advantageous; **-worthy**: trustworthy, cringeworthy; **-proof**: waterproof, foolproof; **-y**: sticky, classy; **-ful**: handful, grateful

Exercise 8
1 1 hospitalised; 2 classify; 3 shortens; 4 widened; 5 beautify

2 **Sample answers: -ise**: economise, legalise; **-en**: slacken, whiten;

-**ify**: simplify, justify;

-**ate**: graduate, duplicate, elongate, accelerate

Pronunciation: Silent letters

Exercise 10

1 Newcastle

2 a /e/ L**eice**ster; R**ea**ding; Gr**ee**nwich

  b /ə/ Leicest**er**; Plym**ou**th

  c /eɪ/ C**a**mbridge

3 ~~Leicester~~ ~~Newcastle~~ ~~Reading~~ ~~Greenwich~~

Exercise 11

1 i**s**land; 2 ca**l**m; 3 cam**e**ra; 4 ha**l**f;

5 int**e**resting; 6 vin**e**yard; 7 wa**l**k;

8 We**d**nesday; 9 forei**g**ner; 10 rest**au**rant

Grammar: The passive

Exercise 13

a My local Italian is said to be the best restaurant in town. / It is said that my local Italian is the best restaurant in town.

b The agent (*my mum*) is known and important so we would not use the passive.

c The new canal has been found to be a flood risk. / It has been found that the new canal is a flood risk.

Exercise 14

Sample answers:

a Although the Lake District is usually considered to be the most beautiful region in the UK, I think Cornwall is just as beautiful.

b Restaurant food is often thought to be superior to home cooking, but, in my opinion, this is far from always the case. My nan is an amazing cook and I'd much rather eat her cooking than eat out.

c It could be argued that it is better to live in the country than in the city, because country life is more idyllic, but I find it ever so boring.

Exercise 15

2 a got (unexpected); b got (achievement);

  c We would probably not use *get* here.

Grammar: The causative

Exercise 16

1 a We're having/getting our lounge repainted.

  b The council had/got a statue of Shakespeare made.

  c I had/got my house burgled.

  d Our house is far too small, so we're going to have/get an extension built.

Exam Technique: Clarifying, paraphrasing and giving examples

Exercise 1

1 Perhaps because they felt that what they had said was too extreme, not reflecting their view precisely enough, and so they wanted to modify/clarify it.

Exercise 2

2 We do not know how big it is but we know that the speaker considers it too small for his family.

10 Culture

Vocabulary: Festivals and historical sites

Exercise 1

1 c; 2 b; 3 d; 4 a

Exercise 2

1 marks; 2 anniversary; 3 celebrations; 4 day off;

5 street parties; 6 banners; 7 national anthem

Exercise 3

1 excavation; 2 remains; 3 unearthed; 4 artefacts;

5 date; 6 BC; 7 primitive; 8 ornaments;

9 construct; 10 draws; 11 finds; 12 exhibited

Pronunciation: Linking

Exercise 7

2 In the first track, the speaker pronounces every word distinctly, and stops between after each word. The speech is slow, lacking in rhythm and does not flow.

3 In the second track, the speaker speaks naturally. Each unit of speech sounds like a flow of sounds, with no pauses.

Exercise 8

2 a /j/

  b /w/

  c /ɪ/, /ɪ/

Exercise 9

Our mo**st** **im**portant festival **is** without doubt Christmas. We /j/ **all** look forward **to** /w/ **it** for months, buying presents fo**r** /ɪ/ **o**ur loved one**s** **a**nd decorati**ng** **ou**r homes. It's magical fo**r** /ɪ/ **ev**eryone but for childre**n** **es**pecially. When we knew Father Christmas wa**s** **ab**out to visit, my sister Samanth**a** /ɪ/ **a**nd I wer**e** /ɪ/ **a**lways t**oo** /w/ **e**xcited to sleep.

Grammar and pronunciation: The future

Exercise 11

2 She uses the present continuous *This year, I'm* ***spending*** *New Year with my boyfriend's family. We're* ***arriving*** *on the 28th of December and* ***staying*** *till the 4th of January. I'm really* ***looking*** *forward to it.*

3 She may have bought her train/plane tickets; she will certainly have arranged with the family when they are arriving and when they are leaving; she might have had to book time off work.

Exercise 13

2 Possible evidence:
   a The team's playing really badly.
   b I can see that she isn't looking where she's going.
   c There are snow clouds and it's really cold.
3 Sentence c

Exercise 15

1 *Are you doing*: It is nearly New Year (Laura talks about finding a 'last-minute deal') so Sarah is most likely to use this tense, presuming Laura has made arrangements already.
2 *I'm going to look*: This is a plan (she talks about having kept the evening free), not an arrangement made with another person.
3 *I'll help*: A spontaneous offer.
4 *Are you going*: It is nearly New Year so Laura is most likely to use this tense, presuming Sarah has made arrangements already.
5 *are spending*: Present continuous is more likely here because, as it is nearly New Year, they must have arranged it with the parents by now.
6 *will be*: A prediction based on an opinion.

Exercise 16

1 will have forgotten

11   On the move

Vocabulary: Holidays

Exercise 1

1 d; 2 a; 3 e; 4 c; 5 b

Vocabulary: Tourism

Exercise 3

1 a environment –; b local people (or economy) +;
c economy +; d local people + (or environment –);

e local people –; f environment –; g economy –;
h environment +

2 a seasonal; b erosion; c unspoilt; d trade

Grammar: Short answers

Exercise 5

1 *Yes, I would* or *No, I wouldn't* + your own answer
2 *Yes, I do* or *No, I don't* + your own answer
3 *Yes, I am* or *No, I'm not* + your own answer
4 *Yes, I have* or *No, I haven't* + your own answer
5 *Yes, I do* or *No, I don't*+ your own answer
6 *Yes, there are* or *No, there aren't* + your own answer
7 *Yes, I did* or *No, I didn't* + your own answer
8 *Yes, I do* or *No, I don't* + your own answer
9 *Yes, I would* or *No, I wouldn't* + your own answer

Expressing yourself indirectly

Exercise 7

1 1 c; 2 g; 3 e; 4 h; 5 f; 6 d; 7 b; 8 a

2 1 a (short/mini) break, a long weekend;
2 sunbathe; 3 a postcard; 4 a youth hostel;
5 flip-flops, sandals; 6 swimming trunks;
7 a toiletry bag, a washbag; 8 a travel agent

Pronunciation: Extra stress

Exercise 10

1 a I WANTed to go but I COULDn't. I was broke. (to contrast two things)
   b Did you say her name was Julie? – No, JuliA. (to correct someone)
   c My HUSband really enjoyed the mini break, but I didn't. (to contrast two things)
   d Was your purse ON the table when it was stolen? – No, it was UNder the table. (to correct someone)

Exercise 11
Sample answers:
1 No, I'm not. I'm from BELgium.
2 No, it has a HOT climate.
3 No, the capital of England is LONdon.
4 No, it lies to the NORTH.

Exercise 12

2 a . . . many people *do* go abroad. . . .
   b . . . we *did* go.
   c I *do* love being able to. . .

Language: Cause and effect

Exercise 13

1 a People have more disposable income than previous generations [C], <u>which means that</u> most people can now afford to go on holiday [E].

b The rapid rise in air travel [E] <u>stems from</u> the creation of low-cost airlines [C].

c Competition between airlines [C] <u>has led to</u> lower prices for passengers [E].

d Staff working for our national airline keep striking [C]. <u>As a result</u>, many people avoid booking with them [E].

e I suffer from seasickness [C] <u>so</u> I never travel by boat [E].

f The severe delays [E] <u>were brought about by</u> the volcanic eruption [C].

2 C = cause; E = effect

Pronunciation chart

In this book the International Phonetic Alphabet (IPA) is used to show how some words are pronounced. The symbols used in the International Phonetic Alphabet are shown in the table below.

IPA Symbols

Vowel	Sounds	Consonant	Sounds
ɑ	calm, ah	b	bed, rub
æ	act, mass	d	done, red
ɑɪ	dive, cry	f	fit, if
ɑɪə	fire, tyre	g	good, dog
ɑʊ	out, down	h	hat, horse
ɑʊə	flour, sour	j	yellow, you
e	met, lend, pen	k	king, pick
eɪ	say, weight	l	lip, bill
eə	fair, care	m	mat, ram
ɪ	fit, win	n	not, tin
i	seem, me	p	pay, lip
ɪə	near, beard	r	run, read
ɒ	lot, spot	s	soon, bus
əʊ	note, coat	t	talk, bet
ɔ	claw, more	v	van, love
ɔɪ	boy, joint	w	win, wool
ʊ	could, stood	x	loch
u	you, use	z	zoo, buzz
ʊə	lure, pure	ʃ	ship, wish
ɜ	turn, third	ʒ	measure, leisure
ʌ	fund, must	ŋ	sing, working
ə	about	tʃ	cheap, witch
		θ	thin, myth
ː	*lengthens the vowel*	ð	then, bathe
	sound	dʒ	joy, bridge